Three UK F-35Bs in formation for Exercise Hightower during the UK Carrier Strike Group deployment, Operation Highmast. MoD/Crown Copyright

AIR POWER
to the fore

Welcome to the *AirForces Monthly Yearbook 2026* which once again highlights events of the past 12 months that made the headlines in the world of modern military aviation.

In this edition we focus on the work of the RAF's Typhoon force, which has been in constant use around the world. Pilots and ground crew have played a significant role in patrolling the skies of Eastern Europe with their deployment to Poland for Operation Chessman, helping to protect NATO's eastern flank during Russia's ongoing war with Ukraine.

On top of that, Typhoons have seen action in Syria, joining forces with France to attack Islamic State targets as part of Operation Shader, which has seen RAF fighters based in Cyprus help in the fight to contain and eradicate terrorist cells and help restore peace to the war-torn state.

The *Yearbook* also showcases the global coverage that appears in each edition of *AirForces Monthly*, with exclusive access to air arms around the world. Of particular note was when *AFM* flew with the Pakistan Air Force and was granted exclusive access to the aircraft that had taken part in the brief conflict with India and assess the claims that they had shot down Indian Air Force Rafale fighters.

Elsewhere we take a look at major exercises such as the UK's flagship event, Cobra Warrior, which saw forces from around the globe gather in Britain for one of the largest fighter exercises the country has ever hosted.

Also featured are some of the iconic combat aircraft still in service around the world. In Turkey they celebrated a milestone for their F-4 Phantom fleet, which still plays a vital role after decades of service. Likewise, we highlight the final units of the Luftwaffe that still fly the venerable Tornado, once the workhorse of the RAF.

Coming right up to date, we takes a detailed look at Britain's aircraft carriers and their deployment last year with the very latest F-35B Lightning II multi-role stealth jets, which are now being operated by both RAF and Royal Navy pilots as British air power returns to the high seas.

The upcoming year will undoubtedly see air power come to the fore with nations uniting against numerous challenges and threats. It looks like it is going to be a very busy, but hopefully peaceful, 2026.

Simon Lee
Publishing Editor
AirForces Monthly

Contents

Cover image
(Front to back): An RAF Typhoon and a Polish Air Force MiG-29 and F-16 during an air-to-air sortie on June 11, 2025, during Operation Chessman.
MoD/Crown Copyright

36

ISBN: 978 1 83632 219 1
Editor: Simon Lee
Senior editor, specials: Roger Mortimer
Email: roger.mortimer@keypublishing.com
Cover Design: Steve Donovan
Design: Key Publishing and SJmagic DESIGN SERVICES, India
Advertising Sales Manager: Sam Clark
Email: sam.clark@keypublishing.com
Tel: 01780 755131
Advertising Production: Becky Antoniades
Email: Rebecca.antoniades@keypublishing.com

SUBSCRIPTION/MAIL ORDER
Key Publishing Ltd, PO Box 300, Stamford, Lincs, PE9 1NA
Tel: 01780 480404
Subscriptions email: subs@keypublishing.com
Mail Order email: orders@keypublishing.com
Website: www.keypublishing.com/shop

PUBLISHING
Group CEO: Adrian Cox
Publisher: Steve O'Hara

Published by
Key Publishing Ltd, PO Box 100, Stamford, Lincs, PE9 1XQ
Tel: 01780 755131 Website: www.keypublishing.com

PRINTING
Precision Colour Printing Ltd, Haldane,
Halesfield 1, Telford, Shropshire. TF7 4QQ

DISTRIBUTION
Frontline Distribution Solutions Ltd,
2 Poultry Avenue, London, EC1A 9PU
Enquiries: 02074 294000 or info@flgroup.co.uk

66

We are unable to guarantee the bona fides of any of our advertisers. Readers are strongly recommended to take their own precautions before parting with any information or item of value, including, but not limited to money, manuscripts, photographs, or personal information in response to any advertisements within this publication.

TYPHOON warning

T his year has seen RAF Typhoons deployed to Poland and the Baltic as part of Operation Chessman, a four-month deployment that ran from March to July 2025. RAF personnel were deployed at Malbork Air Base under the command of the 140 Expeditionary Air Wing (EAW).

On March 26, RAF Typhoons of II Army Cooperation (AC) Squadron from RAF Lossiemouth in Scotland landed at the 22nd Air Base in Malbork, Poland, ahead of enhanced air policing missions as part of NATO's commitment to maintaining regional security and airspace integrity, highlighting the UK's dedication to supporting NATO allies and ensuring the security of Europe.

The RAF has had one of its busiest years in terms of overseas deployments, NATO missions and exercises. At the forefront has been its FGR4 Typhoon multi-role fighters. **Anita Roe** details some of the main activity

An RAF Typhoon, a Polish MiG-29 and a Polish F-16 during an air-to-air sortie over Poland on June 11, 2025. All images MoD/Crown Copyright

The 140 EAW deployment is part of NATO's ongoing air policing programme, which safeguards allied airspace in areas with limited local air defence resources. According to its commending officer, Wing Commander Christopher Jacob: "The arrival of our Typhoon aircraft here at Malbork marks a proud moment for our team as we prepare to take on this vital NATO mission. It is a privilege to be in Poland, a country with which the United Kingdom shares a long and storied history of friendship and co-operation that predates the NATO Alliance. This enduring bond, forged through shared values and mutual respect, reinforces the importance of NATO's collective purpose and strengthens the foundation of our partnership.

II(AC) Sqn Eurofighter Typhoon FGR4 taking off from 22 Tactical Air Base, Malbork, Poland, on July 18, 2025.

No. II (Army Co-operation) Squadron Typhoon departing Malbork at the end of the deployment on August 1.

"We are here to defend and deter, standing ready to protect against any threat, while reassuring our allies of the UK's commitment to NATO and the region. Additionally, we strive to foster partnership, advance interoperability, develop trust and reinforce collaboration and unity among our NATO member partners. Together, we reaffirm our unwavering commitment to NATO's collective defence, safeguarding the skies and fortifying bonds among our allies."

On May 24, two RAF Typhoon FGR4s were scrambled from their deployed operating base in Malbork to intercept a Russian aircraft transiting close to NATO airspace. They discovered an Ilyushin Il-20M, a communications and electronic signals intelligence surveillance-reconnaissance aircraft, with the NATO code name *Coot-A*. The Russian aircraft had been escorted by three other pairs of NATO aircraft earlier that day, but the escort was broken off

A Typhoon from II (Army Co-operation) Squadron preparing to leave its shelter and head to RAF Lossiemouth on August 1, 2025.

aircraft, meaning the NATO aircraft's position cannot be misinterpreted as aggressive.

The spokesperson added: "NATO remains vigilant and ready to safeguard allied airspace 24/7. This is a clear demonstration of the UK's commitment to collective defence."

In June, two RAF Typhoon FGR4s were scrambled for the fourth time in seven days from the 22nd Tactical Air Base in Malbork to intercept unknown aircraft leaving Kaliningrad and approaching NATO airspace. The first three times were to intercept and identify a Russian Ilyushin Il-20M as it left Kaliningrad airspace. On the fourth occasion, NATO scrambled RAF Typhoons to intercept and identify a pair of Russian *Flanker-H*s transiting close to NATO airspace. Aircrew from No. II (Army Co-operation) Squadron, part of 140 EAW, was conducting quick reaction alert (QRA) as part of NATO enhanced air policing (EAP) when it was scrambled.

According to an EAW spokesperson: "Today's mission was to intercept and

when it turned toward Kaliningrad airspace. However, the aircraft then turned and headed southwest towards Polish airspace, which prompted NATO to scramble the Typhoons. It then turned northwest and transited over the Baltic Sea to the north of Poland. Typhoons intercepted the aircraft as it left Kaliningrad airspace and escorted it until it was handed over to the Danish quick reaction alert (QRA).

An EAW spokesperson said: "I was scrambled to intercept the *Coot-A* approaching NATO airspace. Once intercepted, NATO instructed us to escort the aircraft. We escort aircraft to ensure the safety of all airspace users in the vicinity of the non-communicating aircraft. At no point did the aircraft file a flightplan or communicate with civilian air traffic control, and it was also transiting without squawking. Our mission was conducted professionally and in full accordance with international law."

NATO aircraft routinely intercept from the 3 or 9 o'clock position (dictated by weather and the target's direction) relative to the unknown

Two II(AC) Squadron Eurofighter Typhoon FGR4s taxiing at Malbork.

A Russian Air Force Antonov An-30B Clank photographed by an RAF Typhoon pilot. The An-30 is a development of the An-24 designed for aerial cartography.

identify the unknown aircraft departing Kaliningrad airspace. It did not communicate or file a flightplan, which is required under international law. Once intercepted, we escorted the aircraft to protect civilian air traffic in the immediate area, before handing it over to another pair of NATO aircraft."

Since the beginningof June, RAF Typhoons have conducted six NATO enhanced air policing missions in as many days and intercepted 15 Russian aircraft. On June 7, two Typhoon FGR4s were scrambled initially to intercept an unknown aircraft leaving the Kaliningrad Flight Information Region (FIR), encountring an An-30, known by its NATO code name *Clank*, a Soviet-era twin turboprop aerial photography platform. Once the aircraft was identified, the Typhoons shadowed

An RAF Typhoon FGR4 taxiing in front of two Swedish Air Force Gripens on July 15, 2025.

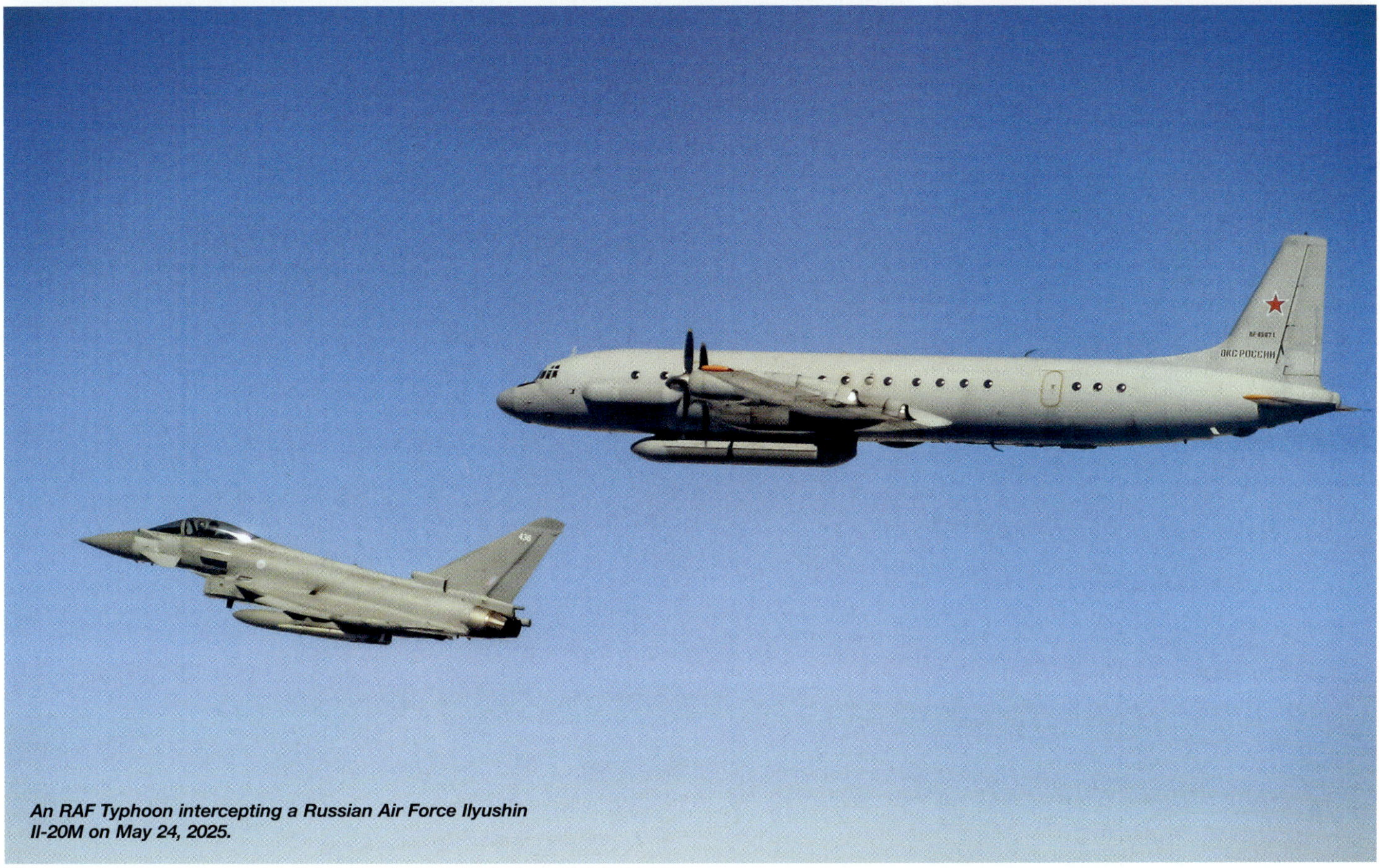

An RAF Typhoon intercepting a Russian Air Force Ilyushin Il-20M on May 24, 2025.

Op Eastern Sentry

RAF Typhoons conducted their first operational sortie under NATO's Eastern Sentry programme, carrying out vigilance activity from September 2025. Two Typhoons from 3 (Fighter) Squadron at RAF Coningsby, supported by a Voyager from 101 Squadron at RAF Brize Norton, patrolled NATO's eastern flank to deter aggression. Vigilance activities are routine defensive operations that demonstrate NATO's ability to respond swiftly to potential threats while maintaining the security of member nations. The RAF Typhoons conducted regular sorties, integrating seamlessly with other NATO air forces.

Air Marshal Allan Marshall said: " NATO's Eastern Sentry mission is to protect NATO airspace and sends a clear message to adversaries that we stand united against any threat to our allies. RAF Typhoons supported by air-to-air refuelling aircraft joined our NATO partners to fortify the eastern flank. This deployment underscored the RAF's readiness and ability to project airpower swiftly and decisively. These missions not only strengthened NATO's air defences, but also served as a deterrent against Russian aggression, all while maintaining the RAF's commitment to defending UK skies and multiple other operational outputs at home and overseas."

UK Defence Secretary John Healey commented: "RAF Typhoons have flown their first air defence missions over Poland, sending a clear signal that NATO airspace will be defended. I'm proud of the outstanding British pilots and air crew who took part in this successful operation to defend our allies from reckless Russian aggression."

RAF Typhoons and Swedish Air Force Gripens training together over the skies of Poland.

the *Clank*, to protect all other aircraft in the vicinity and to ensure optimum safety. NATO then re-tasked the pair to intercept another aircraft – an Ilyushin Il-20M – flying in the same area. Once intercepted and identified, the aircraft was shadowed until it no longer presented a threat.

One of the pilots commented: "Today marked my first operational scramble, and while the adrenaline was high, training took over the moment we launched. Every decision, every movement was second nature thanks to the preparation we've undergone. It was a humbling reminder of the responsibility we carry and the importance of staying sharp and always ready.

"Once our escort of the *Clank* was complete, we were re-tasked to intercept an unidentified aircraft transiting close to NATO airspace. The transition was seamless. The command provided updated vectors and we adjusted our intercept profile accordingly. Intercepting two aircraft in one mission was an intense and eye-opening experience – it reinforced the reality of our role and gave me a new level of respect for the demands of QRA."

Typhoon FGR4s housed in rapid erect shelters (RES) at 22 Tactical Air Base, Malbork, Poland.

The following three days were busy ones for the FGR4s.

On June 8, the aircraft were scrambled to identify two unknown aircraft as they left Kaliningrad FIR. On interception, the RAF pilots identified them as armed Sukhoi Su-24Ms, known by their NATO code name *Fencer-D*, a supersonic, all-weather tactical bomber. Once identified, the pair split, with a Typhoon tasked to escort each aircraft. One *Fencer-D* then conducted low passes over the US navy ship (USNS) *William McLean*.

On June 9, they once again intercepted an Il-20M *Coot-A* and an An-30 *Clank*. Typhoons shadowed both until NATO deemed it was no longer required.

On June 10, the FGR4 aircraft intercepted an Il-20M *Coot-A* for the third time in as many days. The Typhoons then refuelled from a Luftwaffe Airbus A400M Atlas before pursuing another An-30 Clank operating in the area.

NATO then assigned the aircraft to escort a Tupolev Tu-142, known by its NATO code name *Bear-F*, a Russian maritime reconnaissance and anti-submarine warfare aircraft derived from the Tu-95 turboprop strategic bomber. The *Bear-F*, along with a pair of armed Sukhoi Su-27 *Flanker-B*s, were intercepted and shadowed until they were handed over to another pair of NATO air policing aircraft.

An EAW pilot commented: "This was an extremely busy scramble. Over the past few weeks, we have become accustomed to intercepting one aircraft and then being

Typhoon FGR4 using full afterburners as it heads off on a night-time sortie.

Hotpit refuelling of an RAF Typhoon during training in Operation Chessman.

(Closest to furthest): a Polish MIG-29, Polish F-16, an RAF Typhoon and a Swedish Gripen.

(Closest to furthest): an RAF Typhoon, a Polish MiG-29 and a Polish F-16 during an air-to-air sortie on June 11, 2025.

re-tasked to intercept a second. But intercepting a third aircraft in the same sortie is a first for me. While on Operation Chessman, we have trained numerous times with NATO partners, including the German A400M AAR platforms. Today, this training was put into operational use, and with the support of the Luftwaffe we were able to extend our sortie and stay on task as long as NATO required."

A spokesperson for OC No II (AC) Squadron said: "Utilising the AAR platform of our NATO ally has not only extended the effectiveness of our sortie, but also reinforced the strength and trust that defines our alliance. This collaboration exemplifies the power of interoperability, shared capability and mutual support. On behalf of our two aircrew, thank you to our German colleagues for your critical contribution."

Training

On April 12, RAF Eurofighter Typhoons and Swedish Air Force JAS-39 Gripens conducted training together for the first time since the start of their joint deployment to Malbork. The British Typhoons departed first to simulate an adversary formation, with the Swedish Gripens being scrambled to intercept them, supported by a German Air Force A400M air-to-air refuelling aircraft. The sortie allowed pilots from No II (Army Co-operation) and Swedish Air Force 211 and 212 Fighter Squadrons to gain firsthand experience of working together, leading to a better understanding of capabilities and increased interoperability both in the air and among the ground crews.

While this was a first for the detachment, it was not the first time the RAF Typhoons and Swedish Air Force Gripens had trained together. The two countries conducted joint training in October 2022 as part of the Joint Expeditionary Force (JEF) at the Ravlunda Range in southern Sweden.

The officer commanding No. II (AC) Squadron said: "We work to the same

Typhoon FGR4 during a reheat take-off on a QRA practice scamble.

(Closest to furthest): a Polish F-16, an RAF Typhoon and a Swedish Gripen during an air-to-air sortie on the June 11, 2025.

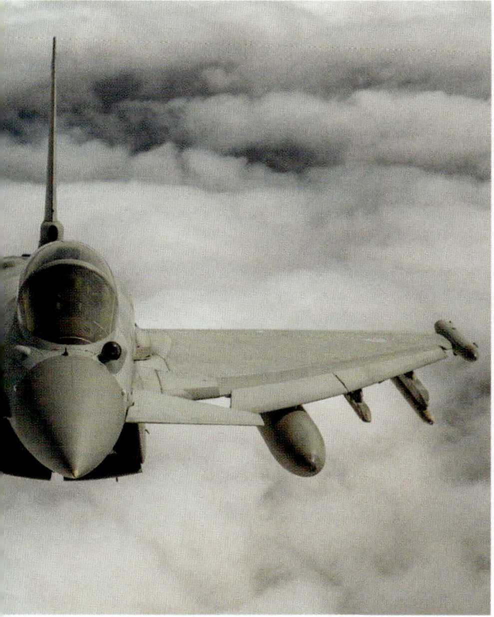

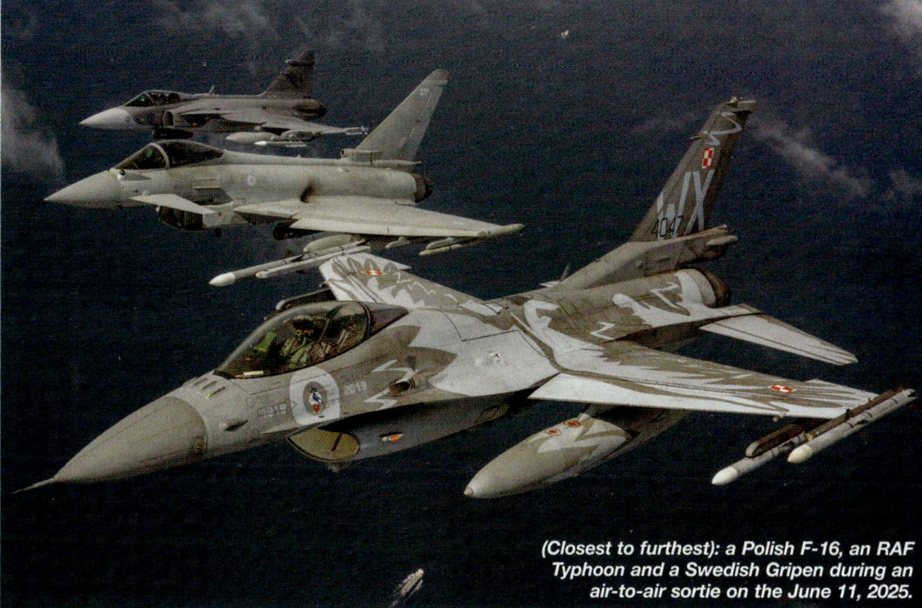

rules and tactics, so it is essential to train with other NATO members. As a pilot, you are always learning, sharing experiences, exchanging tactics and ideas. Ultimately, pilots are all growing and maturing with every mission we fly, whether it is a training sortie or a live mission. Training with other nations and aircraft results in all involved learning new ideas and improving all nations' interoperability. Today was a great experience for all involved."

Conducting air-to-air refuelling from a German A400M was another first for pilots from No. II (AC) Squadron, further enhancing the squadron's capability while operating in the enhanced air policing mission.

One Typhoon pilot commented: "We are greatly experienced in refuelling from RAF Voyager aircraft and similar aircraft from other nations. However, refuelling from an A400M presents unique challenges due to subtle differences, such as airspeed, hose response and basket size and shape. The German crews were extremely professional and it was a great experience working with them."

Exercise Atlantic Trident

Innovation, technological performance and enhancing partnerships with NATO allies – this was the focus for Exercise Atlantic Trident 2025 (Ex AT25) on June 20.

First established in 2010 as part of a trilateral strategic initiative between the UK, US and France, Ex AT25 took place in Finland – a first for this activity – demonstrating NATO's influence and strength in the High North and Finland's deepening integration into the alliance. RAF Typhoon pilots and aircraft engineers from Global Readiness Wing (GRW) at RAF Lossiemouth and the 140 Expeditionary Air Wing (EAW) who were deployed on Operation Chessman in Poland took part, supported by the RAF regiment from 3 Force Protection Wing.

RAF Typhoons preparing to take-off on January 3, 2026, from an undisclosed base in the Middle East as part of operations against IS in Syria.

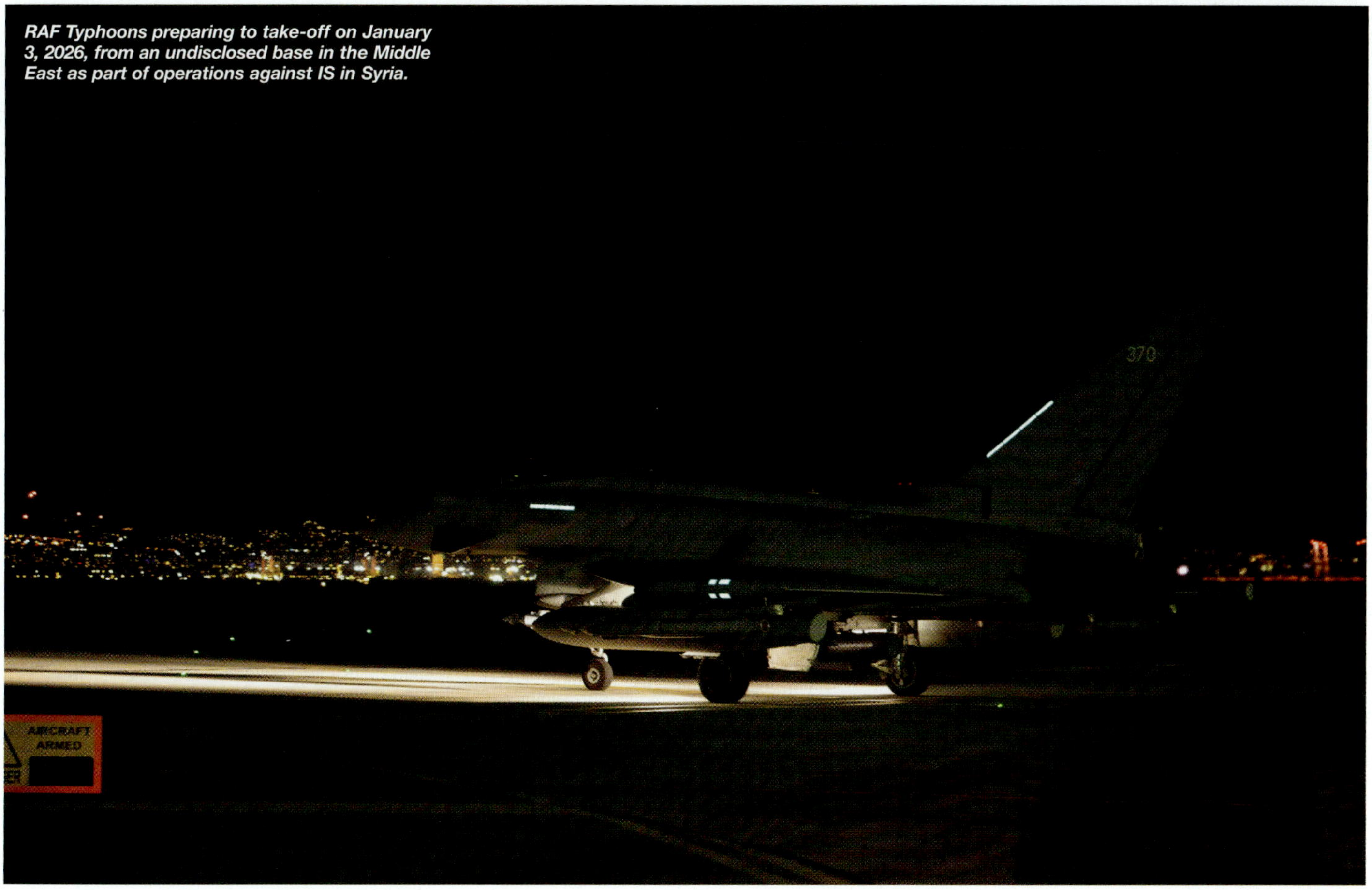

RAF Typhoon operations

Wing Commander Skorge, CO of GRW, said: "Atlantic Trident is more than just a demonstration of airpower. It is a clear message of unity, readiness and resolve. For the Finnish people, this exercise reaffirms NATO's readiness and commitment to collective defence and the principle that we are stronger together."

During the exercise, the aircraft trained together to protect the integrity of an area or territory while operating in an agile combat employment (ACE) environment. ACE training allows all NATO air forces to remain flexible and fast when operating together. This enhances operational integration and combat readiness among NATO allies. Using multiple bases throughout Finland, personnel from all four air forces worked on each other's aircraft, performing minor maintenance tasks such as aircraft refuelling, enabling rapid deployment and turnaround.

Warrant Officer Brown of GRW said: "Exercises like Atlantic Trident matter because they build real trust between personnel on the ground and in the air. For us, it is about making sure we can operate seamlessly with our NATO partners, because when it counts, there won't be time to figure it out. Finland's now fully part of that team, bringing their own experiences and expertise to NATO, and this exercise is about understanding what each partner nation can bring to the fight. We are stronger together, and collective defence starts with working side by side every day."

Exercise Hedgehog Strike

From May 5-23, allied forces demonstrated interoperability and integration during Exercise Hedgehog 25. Canada, Denmark, Finland, France, Germany, Latvia, Poland, Portugal, Romania, Sweden, the UK and the US all participated in Estonia's largest annual military exercise, focused on defensive multi-domain operations. More than 16,000 personnel from the land, sea, and air domains were deployed in support of this large-scale multinational exercise aimed at enhancing interoperability, strengthening NATO's deterrence and defensive capabilities and improving allied readiness to respond to any security challenges.

II(AC) Sqn Eurofighter Typhoon FGR4, during Performance Take Off (PTO) on an evening sortie, on July 17 2025.

A pair of II(AC) Squadron Eurofighter Typhoons embarking on NATO air policing duties.

An RAF Typhoon FGR4 of II Army Co-operation (AC) Squadron from RAF Lossiemouth lands at Malbork Air Base on March 23, 2025, at the start of Operation Chessman.

An RAF Typhoon and Swedish Air Force Gripen being refuelled in the air by a German A400M while on a training sortie.

Typhoons from II (Army Co-operation) Squadron at Lossiemouth deployed to Malbork for NATOs enhanced air policing mission.

Four RAF Typhoon FGR4 fighter jets from NATO's air policing mission in Malbork forward deployed to Estonia to contribute to the exercise. The relocation of these assets highlighted the agility and flexibility of basing options for allied jets in the Baltic region. Sqn Ldr Morrison-Smith, Typhoon detachment commander at Amarï Air Base, said: "This forward deployment of troops from Malbork to Amarï allows us to extend the Typhoons' mission time. Hot pit refuelling allows aircraft to be rapidly refuelled on the ground and returned to the air. This allows us to be an extremely agile force, providing aircraft with the option to refuel via air-to-air tankers or these forward refuelling points that can be established at short notice."

Romanian F-16s from the 'Carpathian Vipers' detachment in Šiauliai, Lithuania, joined the exercise performing close air support (CAS) and air interdiction (AI) within the framework of operations to counter the enemy's surface forces. The air component of the exercise featured an array of aircraft, from the fighter jets to transport helicopters. These assets conducted various missions to simulate real-world scenarios and test the readiness of allied forces. The integration of air assets with ground and naval units underscored NATO's operational cohesion.

NATO's air mobility capabilities were utilised on May 9, when infantry units were moved from Latvia to Estonia using CH-47 Chinook helicopters provided by the RAF. The airlift assets demonstrated the alliance's flexibility in moving personnel and joint logistics to enhance force projection.

The Estonian Defence Forces showcased advancements in their air defence systems during the exercise. The 1st Infantry Brigade achieved combat readiness by integrating new technologies, such as thermal-imaging sights and advanced targeting systems, into its anti-aircraft units. These enhancements, including the deployment of the Mistral missile system, aimed to improve the brigade's ability to counter aerial threats

RAF Typhoon aircraft returning to their base in the Middle East on January 3.

A Typhoon pilot carries out aircraft checks before take-off on January 3, 2026

Britain's Typhoon fleet

The Eurofighter Typhoon has been in service with the RAF since 2003. The current fleet consists of the fourth-generation Typhoon FGR4. A land-based multirole fighter capable of both air-to-air and air-to-ground missions, it forms the bulk of the RAF's combat air fleet alongside the F-35. It also forms the RAF's quick reaction alert force, providing air defence in the UK and across wider NATO airspace when deployed overseas. As of April 1, 2025, the RAF had 129 Typhoons, of which 107 are in service. The aircraft were procured in three tranches and the incremental drawdown of the older Tranche 1 variants began in spring 2025, while later versions are being upgraded to provide more advanced capabilities. The Typhoon will start to leave RAF service in 2040.

The fighter is part of the Eurofighter consortium consisting of BAE Systems, Leonardo and Airbus, which represent the four partner nations – the UK, Spain, Italy and Germany – in the Typhoon project. Development of the Typhoon programme began in the 1980s and production contracts were signed with the Eurofighter consortium in 1998.

In addition to the four partner nations, export orders for the Typhoon have also been secured with Austria (15 aircraft), Saudi Arabia (72 aircraft), Qatar (24 aircraft), Oman (12 aircraft) and Kuwait (28 aircraft). In October 2025, Turkey became the latest country to agree on an export deal for the Typhoon. Following the signing of a memorandum of understanding in July 2025 to strengthen UK-Turkish defence co-operation, Turkey will buy 20 Typhoons in a deal worth £8 billion. It is the UK's first export order for the Typhoon since 2017. Under existing workshare arrangements, 37% of each aircraft will be manufactured in the UK, with final assembly at BAE Systems in Warton. Delivery of the first Typhoon aircraft to Turkey is expected in 2030.

The RAF Typhoons were augmented by a detachment of Swedish Gripen fighters for NATO's enhanced air policing duties.

An RAF C-17 landing at Malbork with supplies and equipment as part of the logistical support for the Typhoon deployment.

effectively. Exercise Hedgehog 2025 served as a preparatory event for the Estonian Division's participation in NATO's Steadfast Deterrence 25 and Griffin Lightning 25 exercises. These exercises focus on strategic deterrence and regional defence planning, with air operations playing a crucial role in ensuring rapid response capabilities and maintaining air superiority in contested environments.

The exercise provided valuable opportunities for NATO air forces to refine their tactics, techniques and procedures through realistic training and operating in a joint and multinational context. Aircrews and ground personnel enhanced their co-ordination, communication and camaraderie. **afm**

Typhoon FGR4 fighter jets forward deployed to Estonia for Exercise Hedgehog Strike 2025.

Sentry duty

The war in Ukraine has created an even greater demand on NATO's E-3A AWACS fleet. **Babak Taghvaee** reports on the challenges and how the US Air National Guard has been called in to help

NATO's ability to maintain persistent airborne surveillance along its eastern flank in 2025 depended on a refuelling architecture that was increasingly strained, fragmented and insufficient to sustain the demanding mission profile of the alliance's ageing E-3A Sentry fleet. The E-3As, operating with fuel-hungry TF33 engines and tasked with multi-hour orbits over Poland, Romania, the Baltic Sea and the Black Sea approaches, required reliable aerial refuelling to remain on station. Yet European tanker capacity – drawn from the USAF's 100th Air Refuelling Wing (ARW) at RAF Mildenhall, the Multinational MRTT Unit based in Eindhoven and Cologne, and periodic French and Turkish contributions – proved unable to meet continuous AWACS requirements.

Heavy national taskings, major exercises and parallel commitments to fighter and transport operations reduced the availability of European tanker fleets for the NATO's E-3A component. At the same time, the component faced its most severe aircraft-availability crisis

A NATO E-3A Sentry receives fuel from a KC-135R of the 351st ARS over Germany on July 17, 2020.
USAF/Tech Sgt Emerson Nuñez

One of NATO's six operational E-3As, LX-N90443, is seen departing Geilenkirchen for a monitoring mission over Lithuania on November 21, 2025.
All images Babak Taghvaee unless stated

On rare occasions, NATO E-3As have participated in exercises outside Europe. Here, E-3A LX-N90447 takes part in the North American Aerospace Defense Command (NORAD) Arctic air defense exercise Amalgam Dart 21-2 on March 24, 2021. *USAF*

As of late 2025, NATO's E-3A component operated between five and six aircraft, conducting a maximum of two monitoring sorties per day over NATO's eastern flank. Here, LX-N90445 is seen departing Geilenkirchen on November 21, 2025.

since its establishment, with seven of the aircraft grounded for long-term modernisation programmes or extended maintenance by late 2025.

Against this backdrop, the United States Air National Guard (ANG) emerged as the indispensable enabler of NATO's airborne early-warning posture. Throughout the year, the ANG deployed 30 KC-135R/T Stratotankers from 14 different air refuelling squadrons to Geilenkirchen AB in Germany, generating 144 sorties in direct support of the E-3A fleet. These deployments provided the predictable, self-sustaining tanker presence that European forces could not supply, allowing NATO to maintain uninterrupted surveillance during periods of acute operational demand – including the response to Russian drone incursions into Polish airspace, the launch of Operation Eastern Sentry following MiG-31BM overflights in Estonia and the high-intensity surveillance environment that followed Russia's expanded strike campaigns in Ukraine.

ANG KC-135R/T fleet

The ANG operates one of the largest and most strategically important aerial refuelling fleets in the United States, fielding 165 KC-135R/T Stratotankers along with 12 recently delivered KC-46As. This force represents nearly half of the air force's total KC-135 inventory and provides a substantial share of the nation's global refuelling capacity. The KC-135 remains the primary refuelling platform for US and allied aircraft worldwide, with the ANG's contribution forming a major portion of the available fleet for overseas operations and rotational deployments.

A defining characteristic of the ANG KC-135 enterprise is its age profile. While the average age of all ANG aircraft is around 27 years, the KC-135T sub-fleet stands out with an average age of more than 60 years,

making it the oldest major aircraft type still flying with the force. Sustaining such an ageing fleet imposes significant logistical and maintenance burdens. Many support systems and maintenance stands date back to earlier decades, requiring replacement or refurbishment. The ANG has had to invest in new maintenance stands, crane and hoist systems and other ground-support equipment to maintain operational safety and

ensure that aircraft availability meets mission requirements.

Although the fleet is ageing, the ANG has implemented several modernisation programmes to preserve the KC-135's mission relevance in demanding and contested environments. A major effort is the integration of large aircraft infrared countermeasures (LAIRCM), which protects the aircraft from shoulder-launched missiles. Wiring kits

A USAF B-52H Stratofortress from the 96th Expeditionary Bomb Squadron flying alongside a NATO E-3A and a KC-135R (63-8028) of the Alaska ANG's 168th ARS over the US European Command area of responsibility, marking a historic first on November 12, 2025. USAF/Staff Sgt Zachary Willis

for the entire fleet are being installed in stages and procurement of LAIRCM pods is advancing, although a significant portion of the requirement remains unfunded.

Another critical upgrade is the real-time information in the cockpit (RTIC) system. This enhancement gives KC-135 crews improved situational awareness and enables the aircraft to interface with modern tactical datalinks. Two aircraft have already demonstrated the system in operational testing, but nearly the entire fleet still awaits modernisation. Both RTIC and LAIRCM represent foundational upgrades that allow the KC-135 to continue operating in modern airspace characterised by dispersed operations, dynamic targeting and elevated threat environments.

Additional modernisation priorities relate to the extreme thermal conditions KC-135 crews encounter during ground operations. Temperatures inside cockpits and cabins can exceed 140°F and 170°F in certain deployed locations, limiting crew endurance and operational effectiveness. Increased investment in ground-cooling systems is thus essential to sustain mission readiness.

Structurally, the KC-135 force is underpinned by long-term recapitalisation planning aligned with the introduction of the KC-46A Pegasus. Current force planning includes the retirement of a limited number of KC-135R/T aircraft as new KC-46s enter service, following a one-for-one replacement strategy. While this transition will take many years, it ensures that the ANG gradually incorporates newer aircraft without degrading overall tanker capacity.

Taken together, the ANG KC-135R/T fleet remains a large, heavily relied-upon and

E-3A LX-N90442 was one of six operational NATO aircraft and flew multiple monitoring missions following Russian drone and aircraft incursions into NATO airspace in September 2025.

The KC-135R/Ts of USAFE's 351st ARS have been used as secondary means of aerial refuelling support for NATO's E-3A fleet.

A USANG KC-135R from the 121st ARW is pushed back to the flight line at Geilenkirchen, Germany, on November 12, 2019, prior to a sortie in support of an E-3A. USANG/Staff Sgt Wendy Kuhn

US Air National Guard KC-135 deployments

Deployment Dates	Serial Number	Type	Unit	Home Base	Sorties	Dates
January 6-14, 2025	58-0010	KC-135R	116th ARS,141st ARW, Washington ANG	Fairchild AFB, Spokane, Washington	3	Jan 7, 8, 14
January 6-14, 2025	59-1520	KC-135T	116th ARS,141st ARW, Washington ANG	Fairchild AFB, Spokane, Washington	3	Jan 8, 10, 13
January 22-21, 2025	59-1458	KC-135R	166th ARS, 121st ARW, Ohio ANG	Rickenbacker ANGB, Columbus, Ohio	4	Jan 24, 28, 29, 30
January 22-21, 2025	62-3511	KC-135R	166th ARS, 121st ARW, Ohio ANG	Rickenbacker ANGB, Columbus, Ohio	4	Jan 27, 28, 29
February 3-14, 2025	59-1446	KC-135R	151st ARS, 134th ARW, Tennessee ANG	McGhee Tyson ANGB, Knoxville, Tennessee	4	Feb 7, 11 (2 sorties), 12
February 3-14, 2025	59-1498	KC-135R	151st ARS, 134th ARW, Tennessee ANG	McGhee Tyson ANGB, Knoxville, Tennessee	2	Feb 6, 12
February 17-28, 2025	57-1435	KC-135R	191st ARS, 151st ARW, Utah ANG	Roland R. Wright ANGB, Salt Lake City, Utah	3	Feb 19, 21, 24
February 17-28, 2025	58-0027	KC-135R	191st ARS, 151st ARW, Utah ANG	Roland R. Wright ANGB, Salt Lake City, Utah	6	Feb 18, 20, 24, 25, 26, 27
March 10-28, 2025	61-0276	KC-135R	173rd ARS, 155th ARW, Nebraska ANG	Lincoln ANGB, Lincoln, Nebraska	6	Mar 12, 17, 20, 21, 25, 27
March 10-28, 2025	62-3526	KC-135R	173rd ARS, 155th ARW, Nebraska ANG	Lincoln ANGB, Lincoln, Nebraska	8	Mar 13, 14, 17, 18, 21, 24, 25, 26
March 31-April 11, 2025	59-1500	KC-135R	108th ARS, 126th ARW, Illinois ANG	Scott AFB, Belleville, Illinois	4	April 1, 2, 3, 4, 9
March 31-April 11, 2025	63-7981	KC-135R	108th ARS, 126th ARW, Illinois ANG	Scott AFB, Belleville, Illinois	7	April 1, 2, 3, 4, 8, 9, 10
May 12-22, 2025	57-2597	KC-135R	151st ARS, 134th ARW, Tennessee ANG	McGhee Tyson ANGB, Knoxville, Tennessee	4	May 13, 14, 15, 20
May 12-22, 2025	59-1509	KC-135R	151st ARS, 134th ARW, Tennessee ANG	McGhee Tyson ANGB, Knoxville, Tennessee	5	May 13, 14, 15, 16, 20
July 8-18, 2025	57-1453	KC-135R	106th ARS, 117th ARW, Alabama ANG	Birmingham ANGB, Alabama	3	July 14, 15, 17
July 8-August 1, 2025	63-8035	KC-135R	106th ARS, 117th ARW, Alabama ANG	Birmingham ANGB, Alabama	5	July 11, 14, 17, 18, 22
July 21-August 1, 2025	57-1473	KC-135R	106th ARS, 117th ARW, Alabama ANG	Birmingham ANGB, Alabama	7	July 22, 23, 24, 25, 29, 30, 31
August 11-21, 2025	58-0109	KC-135R	174th ARS, 185th ARW, Iowa ANG	Colonel Bud Day Field, Sioux City, Iowa	2	August 19, 20
August 11-September 5, 2025	59-1519	KC-135R	174th ARS, 185th ARW, Iowa ANG	Colonel Bud Day Field, Sioux City, Iowa	8	August 18, 19, 20, 26, 29, September 2, 3, 4
August 25-September 5, 2025	62-3566	KC-135R	174th ARS, 185th ARW, Iowa ANG	Colonel Bud Day Field, Sioux City, Iowa	5	August 26, 27, 28, September 3, 4
September 9-26, 2025	61-0290	KC-135R	203rd ARS, 154th Wing, Hawaii ANG	Joint Base Pearl Harbor–Hickam, Honolulu, Hawaii	10	Sep 10, 11, 12, 15, 16, 17, 19, 22, 24, 25
September 8-26, 2025	63-8038	KC-135R	203rd ARS, 154th Wing, Hawaii ANG	Joint Base Pearl Harbor–Hickam, Honolulu, Hawaii	8	Sep 10, 11, 12, 15, 17, 18, 22, 23
September 29-October 10, 2025	57-1462	KC-135R	153rd ARS, 186th ARW, Mississippi ANG	Key Field ANGB, Meridian, Mississippi	2	October 1, 8
September 29-October 10, 2025	60-0341	KC-135R	153rd ARS, 186th ARW, Mississippi ANG	Key Field ANGB, Meridian, Mississippi	2	September 30, October 7
October 20-November 7, 2025	62-3547	KC-135R	117th ARS, 190th ARW, Kansas ANG	Forbes Field ANGB, Topeka, Kansas	8	October 21, 22, 24, 27, 28, 29, 31, November 4
October 21-November 7, 2025	63-8875	KC-135R	117th ARS, 190th ARW, Kansas ANG	Forbes Field ANGB, Topeka, Kansas	5	October 22, 30, November 4, 5, 6
November 10-21, 2025	62-3571	KC-135R	168th ARS, 168th ARW, Alaska ANG	Eielson AFB, Fairbanks, Alaska	6	November 11, 12, 13, 14, 17, 19
November 10-21, 2025	63-8028	KC-135R	168th ARS, 168th ARW, Alaska ANG	Eielson AFB, Fairbanks, Alaska	5	November 12, 13, 14, 18, 20
December 1-12, 2025	57-1419	KC-135R	197th ARS, 161st ARW, Arizona ANG	Goldwater ANGB, Phoenix, Arizona	3	December 2, 4, 8
December 1-12, 2025	62-3516	KC-135R	197th ARS, 161st ARW, Arizona ANG	Goldwater ANGB, Phoenix, Arizona	2	December 5, 10

increasingly stressed force. Its size allows the ANG to sustain global refuelling commitments, but its age demands continual investment in modernisation and maintenance. This combination of capability and strain explains why the ANG plays an indispensable role in supporting NATO's airborne surveillance and air-refuelling requirements – particularly in 2025, when operational tempo along the alliance's eastern flank reached its highest level in decades.

European tankers

European-based tanker forces form the second essential layer of support for NATO's E-3A Sentry operations, complementing the rotational US ANG KC-135R/T deployments to Geilenkirchen. The most heavily tasked among them is the USAF's 351st ARS of the 100th ARW at RAF Mildenhall, whose 17 KC-135R/T aircraft (12 are operational simultaneously) regularly sustain AWACS orbits over Poland, Romania, the Baltic Sea and the Adriatic whenever ANG tankers are not in theatre. However, the wing's permanent commitments – including fighter movements, bomber rotations and theatre logistics – frequently limit the extent to which its aircraft can be dedicated to E-3A support.

The Multinational MRTT Unit (MMU), operating nine Airbus A330-243 MRTT tankers from Eindhoven and Cologne, provides another major source of European refuelling capacity. However, throughout 2025, MMU tankers were heavily committed to supporting German, Dutch and Belgian fighter operations, especially during heightened vigilance periods and major NATO exercises. At times, their limited availability forced NATO to modify AWACS employment, including the forward deployment of E-3As to Šiauliai in Lithuania or Ørland in Norway when Geilenkirchen-based missions could not be sustained by European tankers alone. The French Air and Space Force's A330-243 MRTTs

An image taken from the boom operator's station aboard a KC-135R of the USANG's 121st ARW as it refuels a NATO E-3A over Germany on November 14, 2019. USANG/Staff Sgt Wendy Kuhn

The farthest deployment to Europe by a USANG KC-135 unit in support of NATO's E-3A component was conducted by the 203rd ARS of the 154th Wing, Hawaii ANG – KC-135R 63-8038 was one of two aircraft deployed to Geilenkirchen in September 2025.

and, in rare cases, Turkish KC-135Rs also contributed episodically when national schedules allowed, offering limited supplemental capacity rather than steady, predictable support.

These recurring shortages in European tanker availability had a direct operational effect on the E-3A component, especially during a year in which the fleet was severely constrained by modernisation and maintenance. By December 2025, only a handful of the aircraft were operational at Geilenkirchen: LX-N90444, LX-N90445, LX-N90448, and LX-N90453 were active and flying missions, while LX-N90442 and LX-N90443 had entered extended

NATO E-3A Sentry

The USANG's 108th ARS deployed two KC-135Rs, including 59-1500, to Geilenkirchen between March 31 and April 11, 2025. This aircraft logged four sorties.

maintenance in November and LX-N90451 remained under organizational repair. Six aircraft – LX-N90446, LX-N90447, LX-N90450, LX-N90452, LX-N90454, and LX-N90456 – were absent from operations due to long-term upgrades at Manching or Venice. Only LX-N90459 had recently completed its upgrade and was undergoing post-modernisation trials. In effect, less than one-third of the E-3A fleet remained mission-ready at the end of the year.

With so few airframes available, each sortie had to remain airborne for the maximum possible duration, which increased dependence on reliable tanker support. Because the E-3A is equipped with fuel-hungry Pratt & Whitney TF33-PW-100A engines, uninterrupted refuelling is not optional – it is what enables the aircraft to maintain long surveillance lines over the eastern flank. But the competition for European tanker hours, especially from fighters and transport missions, meant that NATO could not depend on Europe-based tankers alone to sustain these demanding operations. As a result, the ANG's rotational KC-135 deployments became not merely helpful but operationally indispensable, filling gaps that European fleets could not cover consistently throughout the year.

ANG to the rescue

The reliance on ANG's KC-135R/T Stratotankers to support NATO's E-3A Sentry missions is the direct result of structural limitations within Europe's tanker ecosystem combined with the operational requirements of the AWACS fleet. The E-3A remains powered by TF33-PW-100A engines, which consume significantly more fuel than modern turbofan engine, so require frequent aerial refuelling to sustain long-duration surveillance orbits over Poland, Romania, the Baltic Sea and the Black Sea. Because NATO's AWACS missions must often remain on station for

extended periods to monitor Russian military activity, refuelling support is not optional, it is an operational prerequisite. Throughout 2025, this requirement collided with the reality that European tanker resources were consistently oversubscribed.

The 100th ARW at RAF Mildenhall provides the bulk of routine US tanker coverage in Europe, but its KC-135R/T fleet must simultaneously support missions of the 48th and 52nd Fighter Wings in Spangdahlem and RAF Lakenheath respectively, bomber task force deployments, logistic refuelling demands and US strategic commitments across multiple theatres. As a result, its availability for AWACS operations fluctuates and is often limited. The Multinational MRTT Unit, operating A330 MRTTs from Eindhoven and Cologne, faces similar constraints. Its aircraft were heavily tasked in 2025 by German, Dutch and Belgian

fighter operations and major NATO exercises, leaving minimal capacity to sustain the E-3A component. Episodic contributions from French A330 MRTTs and Turkish KC-135Rs helped relieve pressure but were not predictable or frequent enough to provide consistent coverage.

These chronic shortfalls in European tanker availability directly shaped NATO's operational decisions throughout the year. On several occasions, the E-3A Component was forced to adjust its basing and deployment pattern, not because of security concerns, but because European tanker assets could not guarantee the refuelling needed for missions originating at Geilenkirchen. This effect was evident in April 2025, when three E-3As were deployed to Šiauliai and two others to Ørland. The decision was driven by the lack of available MMU tankers, which were committed to

The 168th ARS of the Alaska ANG deployed two KC-135Rs to Geilenkirchen AB between November 10 and 21, 2025, with 63-8028 logging five sorties during this deployment.

Among the 30 USANG KC-135s deployed to Germany in 2025, this aircraft from the 203rd ARS of the Hawaii ANG logged the highest number of sorties: ten between September 9 and 26.

exercise Ramstein Flag 2025 from March 31 to April 11 and fighter operations, leaving the AWACS fleet without the support required to sustain missions over the eastern flank from their home base.

Compounding these tanker limitations was the reduced operational strength of the E-3A fleet itself. By December 2025, modernisation cycles, extended maintenance and organisational repairs had removed the majority of the fleet from active service, leaving only a few aircraft capable of flying missions. With so few airframes to hand, each sortie had to achieve maximum endurance to prevent gaps in NATO's surveillance posture. This placed even greater dependence on tankers, making uninterrupted refuelling support indispensable. Without guaranteed tanker capacity, NATO risked losing persistent real-time coverage of Russian military activity and drone operations near alliance borders.

The ANG filled this gap because it is the only source of additional tanker capacity that can be deployed rapidly, sustained for weeks at a time and scheduled in predictable rotational cycles without degrading other ongoing missions. ANG KC-135s bring their own crews, maintenance teams and logistical support, allowing them to operate autonomously from Geilenkirchen and integrate seamlessly into the E-3A component's weekly tasking. Their presence ensures that surveillance missions can be flown to full duration even when European tankers are occupied with national or multinational commitments. In practice, the ANG has become the stabilising element of NATO's AWACS aerial refuelling structure, the only resource that can reliably fill gaps created by Europe's tanker shortages and the operational demands placed on the remaining E-3A fleet.

By 2025, this reliance was no longer occasional but structural. Without ANG KC-135 deployments, NATO would not have been able to maintain uninterrupted airborne early-warning coverage during major events such as Russian drone incursions into Poland, Operation Eastern Sentry or periods of heightened Russian military activity across the Baltic and Black Sea regions. The ANG's tankers enabled mission continuity at a time when E-3A availability was at its lowest and European tanker capacity was stretched to its limits. Their role has become essential not only for extending flight endurance but also for safeguarding NATO's surveillance posture during the most volatile security environment Europe has faced in decades.

Deployments to Geilenkirchen

Throughout 2025, the ANG conducted the most extensive series of tanker rotations

This USANG KC-135R, 63-7981 of the 108th ARS, at Geilenkirchen in April 2025 is famous for its World War Two-style recognition markings.

NATO E-3A fleet

S/N	C/N	Current Status	Delivery Date	Operating place in December 2025
LX-N90442	22855/945	Under maintenance	January 22, 1982	Under maintenance at Geilenkirchen since November 4, 2025.
LX-N90443	22838/947	Under maintenance	May 19, 1982	Under maintenance at Geilenkirchen since November 21, 2025.
LX-N90444	22839/949	Active	August 19, 1982	Operational at Geilenkirchen.
LX-N90445	22840/951	Active	November 12, 1982	Operational at Geilenkirchen.
LX-N90446	22841/953	Under modernization	March 10, 1983	Under modernization at Venice since June 7, 2023.
LX-N90447	22848/964	Under modernization	June 5, 1983	Under modernization at Manching since December 8, 2021.
LX-N90448	22843/956	Active	June 27, 1983	Operational at Geilenkirchen.
LX-N90450	22845/959	Under modernization	October 12, 1983	Under modernization at Manching since June 15, 2023.
LX-N90451	22846/961	Under repair	January 20, 1984	Under organizational level maintenance at Geilenkirchen since September 12, 2024.
LX-N90452	22847/963	Under modernization	April 27, 1984	Under modernization at Venice since February 29, 2024.
LX-N90453	22848/964	Active	May 18, 1984	Operational at Geilenkirchen.
LX-N90454	22849/966	Active	November 2, 1984	Under modernization at Manching since March 13, 2025.
LX-N90456	22851/968	Under modernization	November 17, 1984	Under modernization at Venice since December 2, 2024.
LX-N90459	22854/971	Under trial	April 30, 1985	Passing post-modernization tests at Geilenkirchen since October 25, 2024.

ever undertaken in support of NATO's E-3A component, deploying 30 different KC-135R/ Ts from 14 air refuelling squadrons across the US. These missions ensured uninterrupted AWACS coverage during a year marked by heightened Russian activity, major NATO exercises and severe reductions in the operational availability of the E-3A fleet due to modernisation and maintenance. Each ANG rotation lasted between two to three weeks, during which each KC-135 took part in no fewer than four sorties but frequently exceeded ten, depending on mission intensity and the availability of European-based tankers. This amounted to more than 160 sorties flown directly in support of NATO's airborne early-warning missions, enabling the E-3As to sustain long-endurance orbits over the eastern flank.

The first rotations of the year began in early January, when two aircraft from the 116th ARS of the Washington ANG – KC-135R 58-0010 and KC-135T 59-1520 – arrived at Geilenkirchen and flew a total of six sorties supporting AWACS missions over Poland and the Baltic region. Later in January, the 166th ARS of the Ohio ANG deployed KC-135Rs 59-1458 and 62-3511, flying eight sorties between them during a period of intensified monitoring of Russian activity near Kaliningrad and Belarus. In February, two aircraft from the 151st ARS of the Tennessee ANG – 59-1446 and 59-1498 – continued the support effort, conducting six sorties as NATO surveillance flights increased in anticipation of Russian drone and cruise-missile activity.

Later in February, the 191st ARS of the Utah ANG deployed KC-135Rs 57-1435 and 58-0027. The latter aircraft alone flew six sorties, reflecting a spike in mission requirements as the E-3As expanded their surveillance footprint over Romania and the Black Sea approaches. In March, the Nebraska ANG's 173rd ARS arrived with KC-135Rs 61-0276 and 62-3526, which collectively flew 14 missions, marking one of the highest-tempo rotations of the year. This period coincided with Russia's intensified long-range strike activity against Ukraine and increased NATO vigilance along the eastern flank.

A critical deployment occurred from March 31 to April 11, when two KC-135Rs from the 108th ARS of the Illinois ANG – 59-1500 and 63-7981 – were dispatched to Geilenkirchen during Exercise Ramstein Flag and a major AWACS surge. Their combined 11 sorties were essential because MMU A330 MRTTs

An image taken onboard a KC-135R of the USAF's 351st ARS during a mission in support of a NATO E-3A over Spain on July 2, 2025.
USAF/Airman 1st Class Aidan Martínez

KC-135R 62-3516 of the Arkansas ANG's 197th ARS, one of two aircraft deployed to Germany in December 2025, carried a commemorative sticker honouring fallen members of the US armed forces.

the fleet's operational availability had sharply declined due to heavy modernisation work.

By the end of 2025, the operational necessity of these deployments was unmistakable. With most E-3As unavailable – either undergoing modernization at Manching and Venice or grounded in long-term maintenance at Geilenkirchen – the component depended on the endurance that only reliable tanker support could provide. European tanker fleets, heavily tasked by their own national requirements, could not deliver this continuity. The ANG alone provided the predictable, high-tempo tanker presence required to keep NATO's AWACS missions airborne. In a year defined by unprecedented Russian drone incursions, escalating regional tensions and a severely reduced E-3A fleet, the ANG's KC-135 deployments became the indispensable factor that preserved NATO's uninterrupted airborne surveillance posture across the eastern flank. **afm**

were heavily committed elsewhere, forcing the E-3A component to rely almost entirely on ANG tankers for its weekly operational lines. The absence of a planned follow-on ANG rotation in late April directly contributed to NATO's decision to forward-deploy three E-3As to Šiauliai and two others to Ørland, as tanker coverage from Geilenkirchen could no longer be guaranteed.

Support resumed on May 12-22 with Tennessee ANG aircraft 57-2597 and 59-1509, which generated nine sorties as NATO conducted expanded surveillance following Russian drone incursions into Poland. In July, the Alabama ANG's 106th ARS sent three aircraft – 57-1453 (replacement), 63-8035, and 57-1473 – flying a combined 15 sorties during a period of sustained regional tension and intensified training activity. The year's final major deployment occurred between mid-August and early September, when two aircraft from the Iowa ANG's 174th ARS – 58-0109 and 59-1519 – supported the E-3A component with ten sorties at a time when

The final USANG KC-135Rs supporting NATO's E-3A component in 2025 were 57-1419 and 62-3516 from the 197th ARS of the 161st ARW, Arkansas ANG, from December 1-12, 2025.

The final two USANG KC-135Rs supporting NATO's E-3A component in 2025 departed Geilenkirchen AB on December 12, 2025, including 57-1419 of the 197th ARS.

SYNCHRONISING
air power

Cobra Warrior 25-2, the UK's largest air exercise of the year, took place recently. **Dylan Eklund** went along to talk to some of the participants

Dramatic head-on shot of a pair of 425 TFS CF-188 Hornets over the North Sea Department of National Defence, Cpl Bélynda Casse

The latest iteration of the biannual Cobra Warrior exercise commenced at RAF Waddington on September 15. The central premise of the exercise remains the culmination of what the RAF considers some of the highest and best training available over the preceding several months to their weapons instructors.

The long-standing Qualified Weapons Instructor (QWI) course has developed into an attractive opportunity for partner nations to achieve their own training objectives, in turn providing breadth, depth and complexity unachievable when solely an event for UK participants.

Group Captain Paul Hanson, head of operations and training at the Air and Space Warfare Centre (ASWC) was exercise director for Cobra Warrior 25-2. Asked to describe the drills, the former Typhoon pilot said: "It is certainly one of the largest and most complicated air exercises delivered in Europe, and probably one of the most integrated in the world. "

Preparation

Prior to the commencement of the exercise, operators have mastered their own aircraft. Cobra Warrior brings them together in a live environment and in a multi-national force which includes both naval and ground units plus cyber and space domains.

Gp Capt Hanson said: "At one level it is the culmination of our weapons instructor training, a nine-month process where we take the very best people off the frontline from all of our aircraft we fly, and make them the most exceptional instructors, tactical leaders and tactical advisers as we possibly can. We take these tactical experts and turn them into people who can fuse, sequence and synchronise effects across everything, so that the sum of all the parts that are at play equals something you can get advantage from, in a time and space of your

choosing, so you can deliver decisive effects through air power."

While air focused, the exercise is inherently joint, integrated and international in nature, according to Gp Cpt Hanson: "The aim in constructing these exercises is to see what overall objectives we can achieve and how are we going to get through some of the most complicated situations we might face. So we look at the highest levels of threats we're likely to face, both in the air and on the ground. How do we deal with electronic warfare and fight through to gain a position of advantage to achieve our objectives?"

Once they earn the QWI qualification, students return to their respective squadrons to lead operations around the world. These now include Poseidon MRA1 personnel who were participating in the exercise for the first time.

With each iteration of the exercise comprising air arms and aircraft types from different nations, inevitably no two Cobra Warrior exercises are the same. But while the RAF QWI training is central, and the format of two weeks of regular flying and a final week of night flying remain consistent, the scenarios do differ.

Airspace

The ASWC is proud of the airspace structure available for the exercise missions. Being one of the largest exercise areas in Europe, the full spectrum of effects can be employed even though much of it is over the sea. In the exercise area, aircraft can drop chaff and flares and go supersonic when required. The area is also large enough to simulate Meteor v Meteor missile engagements not available at other events.

For Cobra Warrior 25-2 the focus was on air-land integration. This included 300 troops across northern England operating on private land away from their traditional military training ranges. Elements of 16 Air Assault Brigade and US Pathfinders conducted a live parachuting exercise from RAF Atlas C1 and an RAF Mildenhall based MC-130J as part of an early training serial. Airborne helicopter assaults were also conducted from RAF Chinooks.

Although the RAF heralded the event on social media as the UK Air Defence Exercise, the training objectives were, in fact, offensive. Thus, countering enemy drones was not a factor, although there was some integration between crewed and uncrewed platforms by ground forces operating on the RAF Spadeadam electronic warfare range, which also provided high end surface-to-air missile replicators.

In addition to eight Luftwaffe EF2000s at RAF Waddington, a number of units participated from their home stations, including RAF air mobility assets at RAF Brize Norton and F-15E and F-35A from the 48th Fighter Wing at RAF Lakenheath.

Debrief

After each exercise sortie, participants were able to dial in over classified means from their operating locations and see both the fight in real-time and then watch the debrief in what was described as a 'classified Zoom call'.

Gp Capt Hanson explained: "Individuals can see what part they played in their particular part of the mission but also see the bigger picture. This level of training really pushes our tactical experts to be better. The learning environment in the debrief is just phenomenal –

it's honest and transparent. Each nation is learning from the others and really improving everybody's knowledge and understanding."

USAF heavy metal

Two B-52H Stratofortresses participated in the first two weeks of the exercise. Operating from RAF Fairford by the 93rd Bomb Squadron, the Air Force Reserve unit

B-52H Stratofortress 61-0014/OT was one of two examples deployed to RAF Fairford, this one is sporting markings for the Barksdale AFB based 49th Test & Evaluation Squadron Dylan Eklund

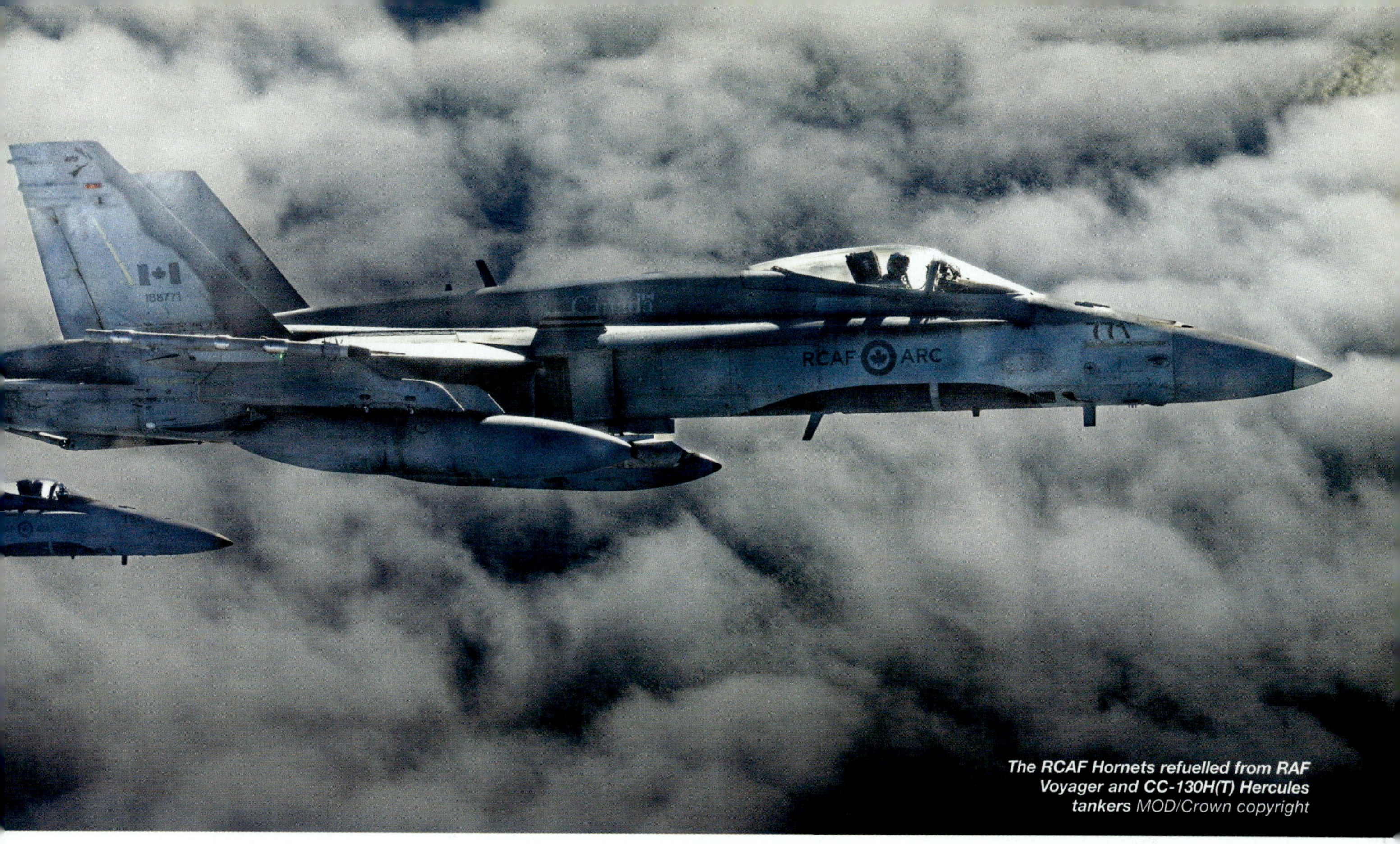

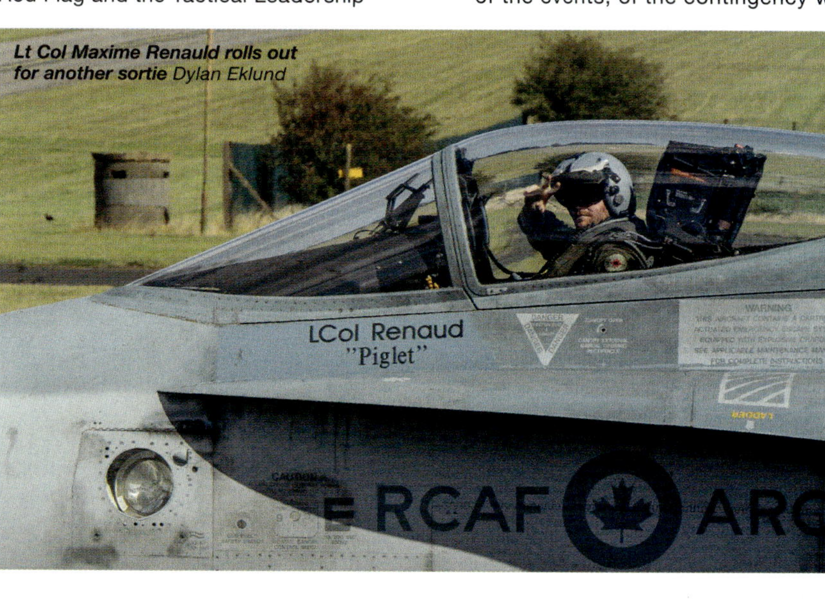

The RCAF Hornets refuelled from RAF Voyager and CC-130H(T) Hercules tankers *MOD/Crown copyright*

deployed with a jet from the co-located 49th Test and Evaluation Squadron, a rare appearance by an operational test aircraft in Europe (see also Ostrava show report, *AFM*, October 2025, p90-93).

Gp Capt Hanson commented: "It's great for the exercise to have B-52s taking part and integrating some of the longer-range weapons and variety of weapons. It's been a great headache for our students to unlock, and very representative about how we might fight in the future. It's also brilliant for us as team leaders trying to integrate a system that carries that much capability and munitions.–

"It's a challenge for us as exercise designers to be able to incorporate that, but it's a brilliant bit of exposure so that when we send people out on live operations, not only to fly for themselves but also going into headquarters, they're going to have to learn how to integrate these things as future instructors and leaders"

The B-52s flew single ship sorties during the exercise, returning home to Barksdale AFB on September 25.

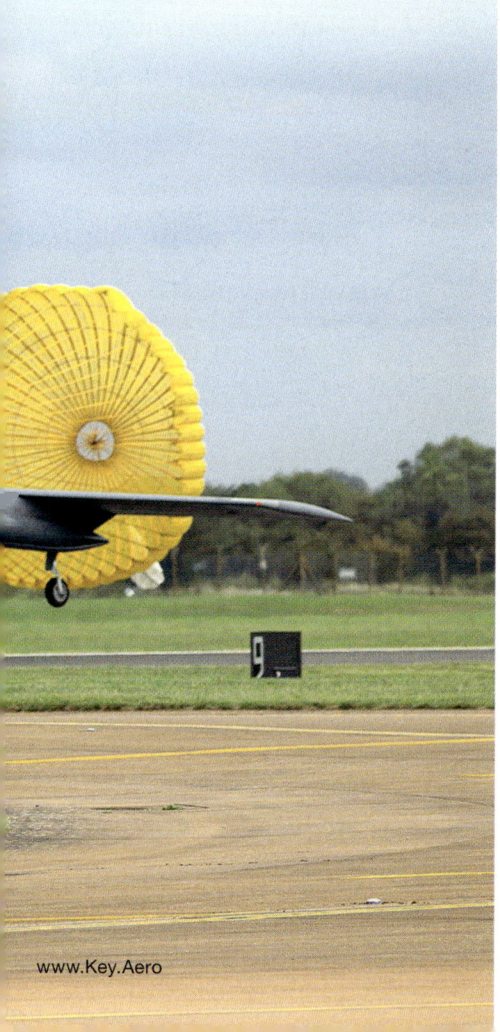

Tier one training

Cobra Warrior is one of three large air exercises the RAF participates in where personal development is to the fore, namely Red Flag and the Tactical Leadership Programme (TLP).Gp Capt Hanson elaborated: "The format is roughly the same as TLP, which is a format dedicated for element lead pilots, so less experience is required than to conduct a mission here. This is more a Red Flag format, but the main difference is that the expertise levels are really high. Red Flag is something in between TLP and Cobra Warrior in terms of training audience.

"The focus of Cobra Warrior is more on integration than other exercises. We attend Red Flag every year and without doubt working with high-tier US capability is vital to our own development and understanding of how a key ally works. The TLP is also vital as for how we work with European allies, but what you get with Cobra Warrior is a sense of integration across all the domains.

"The realism between the exercises doesn't change much, it's just the difficulty of the events, of the contingency which can

Lt Col Maxime Renauld rolls out for another sortie *Dylan Eklund*

RCAF Hornets wait for a 12 Squadron Typhoon and take their turn to refuel from an RAF Voyager tanker MOD/Crown Copyright

be given to the training audience, or the tactical problem and deep analysis that is requested to solve the problem that can arise in the exercise."

Canadian participation

The Royal Canadian Air Force (RCAF) is no stranger to Cobra Warrior, this year deploying eight CF-188 Hornets and a CC-130H(T) to RAF Waddington.

The RCAF Detachment Commander was Lieutenant Colonel Maxime Renaud, commanding officer of 425 Tactical Fighter Squadron (TFS) 'Alouettes'. Hornet pilot

Renaud, callsign 'Piglet', has over 3,000 flying hours (1,900 on the Hornet) to his credit. He explained the context of the deployment: "Cobra Warrior is part of Op Reassurance, Canada's response to what happened in Crimea in 2014. It's the biggest operation we have overseas right now and has a couple of tiers. The first is to reassure our allies, mostly in central and eastern Europe, that we are there for them as part of NATO, and also to prove to Russia that we can deploy and project force to Europe from Canada to deter further aggression. Integration with European allies in large force employment exercises

is our main objective. So integrating into all the mission sets that we're trained for back home on a smaller scale, we come here and integrate into the NATO force package."

The Canadian deployment included members of fellow CFB Bagotville-based 433 TFS. "We have our most experienced pilots in 3 Wing at Bagotville with us, and we also have some of our most junior pilots. It's important to give experience to the whole of the squadron so that everyone is ready to work with our NATO allies."

The CC-130H(T) that flew air-air refuelling sorties each day came from CFB Winnipeg-based 435 Transport and Rescue Squadron: "We wanted to bring a tanker here to extend our mission time, but also in case our allies needed gas, so they can use it as well."

Mission commanders

Although the RCAF did deploy with their own fighter weapons instructors (FWIs) they did not use the exercise to qualify new ones. However, the opportunity was taken to meet the 425 TFS objective of qualifying three mission commanders. The RCAF does not run FWI courses every year, so Cobra Warrior provided a convenient opportunity to run a mission commander course – the first since 2023.

Prior to arrival in the UK, students undertook ground school and academic lectures with Cobra Warrior acting as their graduation exercise, the FWIs administering the check ride for the prospective mission commanders. On qualification, each mission commander is ready to lead large force employment packages.

A Hornet approaching a CC-130H(T) Hercules tanker Department of National Defence, Cpl Bélynda Casse

TLG 74 at Neuberg deployed eight Eurofighters to RAF Waddington Chris Wood

Tarassis

On conclusion of Cobra Warrior, the RCAF detachment deployed to Estonia for Exercise Tarassis, a Joint Expeditionary Force led exercise. Lt Col Renauld said: "For us, it's a proof of concept for agile concept employment – one of a series of exercises we'll do in both Europe and Canada to further develop the concept."

Ahead of that exercise, the RCAF liaised with the Finnish Air Force regarding operating from unprepared airstrips (see Finnish Air Force Commander interview, p86-90). Lt Col Renaud said: "We've been keen to understand the considerations: how they brief it, how they approach landing on strips because it's not like landing on a runway. There's many more considerations that we may not be aware of, so we've been closely working with them."

Cobra Warrior 26-1

The next exercise, Cobra Warrior 26-1 in spring 2026, will have more of a defensive counter-air focus, with a much heavier air-maritime emphasis. While only a couple of small ships took part in 25-2, the ASWC hopes next year to have a Royal Navy Type 45 destroyer, Type 23 frigate and Royal Marines commandos participating. According to Gp Capt Hanson: "The idea is we cover all the bases in detail and build toward being part of a series of much larger NATO exercises in 2027."

Aeronautica Militare

The Aeronautica Militare deployed six Eurofighter F2000As to RAF Coningsby, some 15 miles east of Waddington, where they worked closely with the weapons school at 29 Squadron. The aircraft were drawn from four different wings: the 4° Stormo at Grossetto, 36° Stormo at Gioia del Colle, 37° Stormo at Trapani and 51° Stormo from Istrana.

A Major with 36° Stormo, callsign 'Cavallo', explained his nation's participation in the exercise: "We're here to upgrade, train and qualify weapons instructors. After qualification, they'll be back in their respective unit and squadron and will be the key representative in the role of tactical mentor. This also ensures standardisation between all the units."

A Eurofigher pilot with 2,000 hours on type since 2012, 'Cavallo' explained that the selection for weapons instructor was based not only on performance on the ground and in the air, but also other specific criteria, with great weight placed on personal attributes: "Attitude and commitment are the main characteristics we look for. You should be humble, approachable and you have to be ready to improve your knowledge and, most importantly, be prepared to share this knowledge.

"We test their ability to plan, brief, conduct and debrief a complex mission in a high intensity scenario. That requires analysis of a tactical problem in a multi-domain scenario

Above: Commanding officer of 425 TFS and RCAF detachment commander for Cobra Warrior 25-2, Lt Col Maxime Renauld Dylan Eklund

in order to be ready tomorrow to deter any evolving threat. It's quite challenging. It's really high level in terms of expertise and you need to be able to plan alongside our allies. We can share knowledge and improve understanding and, as a consequence, improve our interoperability." **afm**

The Italian Air Force deployed Eurofighters F-2000As from a mix of units to RAF Coningsby Chris Wood

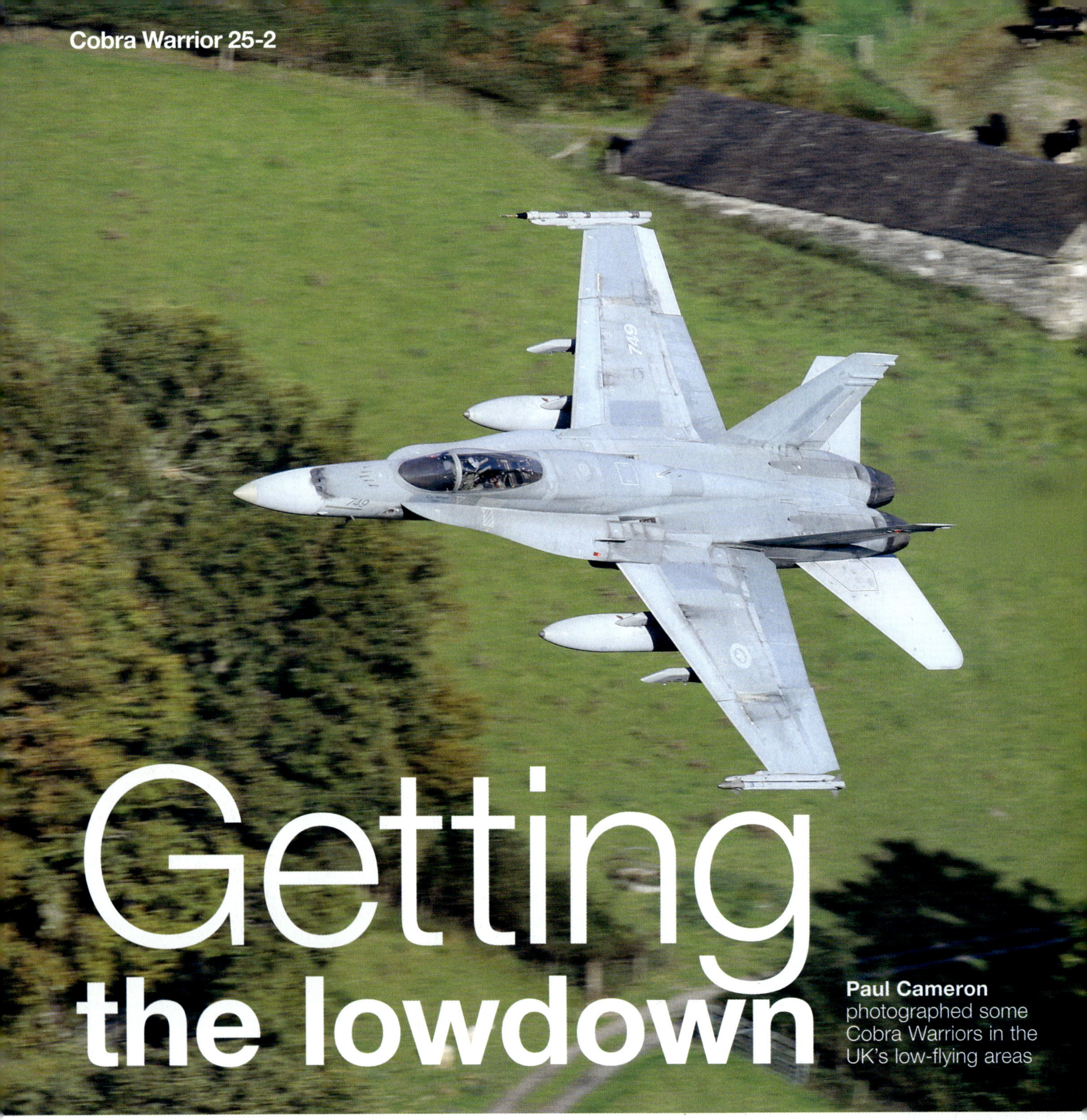

Getting the lowdown

Paul Cameron photographed some Cobra Warriors in the UK's low-flying areas

The latest iteration of the RAF's biannual Cobra Warrior Exercise played host to Canada, Germany, Italy and the United States from September 15 to October 3. RAF Waddington was to base for the Canadian and German participants, while RAF Coningsby was the temporary home for the Italian participants.

Most of the aircraft from all nations involved in the exercise took the opportunity to make use of the UK's extensive low-fly networks at some point during their stay. The German and Italian Air Force participated with Eurofighter EF-2000s and were seen mainly utilising the low fly areas of Cumbria (LFA 17), while the Canadian's in their CF-188 Hornets and a single CC-130H Hercules headed for North Wales (LFA 7) including the famous 'Mach Loop'.

During the second week of the exercise, the Canadian CF-188's were seen every day due to the good weather providing excellent conditions for low level flight. Here are a few images captured from one of those days, including some USAF F-15E Strike Eagles from 48th FW at RAF Lakenheath. **afm**

An F-15E Strike Eagle 91-0603/'LN'from the 494th Fighter Squadron 'Black Panthers' of the 48th Fighter Wing passes by a recently felled forest

Royal Canadian Air Force CF-188 Hornet, 188749, 'SCAR23' against a typical Welsh Valley setting All photos, author unless stated

Above: Using the callsign 'SCAR21', this Royal Canadian Air Force CF-188 Hornet, 188734, from 425 Tactical Fighter Squadron leads a flight of four through the 'Mach Loop'

Below: An RAF Lakenheath-based F-15E Strike Eagle, 96-0204/'LN', from the 494th FS 'Black Panthers' makes a hard turn through the valley. It's one of the few aircraft still carrying colourful nose art from a recent Middle East deployment

A German Air Force twin-seat Eurofighter from Taktisches Luftwaffengeschwader 74 Dino Carrera

The Italian Air Force sent six Eurofighters from four different Stormos. This one wears the marking of the newest one, 51 Stormo, based at Istrana Dino Carrera

F-15E Strike Eagle 00-3004/'LN'of the 494th FS 'Black Panthers' down low in LFA 7 in Wales

Bison bids farewell

After six decades serving the Indian Air Force, the MiG-21 has finally been stood down. **Atul Chandra** spent three days at Air Force Station Chandigarh to witness the retirement of the last MiG-21UPG Bison.

The Indian Air Force (IAF) pulled out all the stops to ensure that one of its most important combat types received a fitting send-off at Air Force Station (AFS) Chandigarh on September 26, when the 28 Squadron 'Panthers' – the last IAF squadron to operate the MiG-21 'Bison' – said farewell.

The earliest MiG-21 variant, the MiG-21F-13 (Type-74), was delivered to the IAF in 1963 and since then, the IAF acquired 872 MiG-21s across various variants; India's state-owned aerospace company Hindustan Aeronautics Limited (HAL) producing nearly 600 examples of the type under licence from the MiG design bureau.

Between 1966 and 1987, large-scale induction of various MiG-21s provided the IAF with quantity and quality. The service operated its MiG-21 variants in interceptor, ground attack and trainer roles, to name a few.

The formal decommissioning ceremony was marked by a large gathering of veterans who arrived to say goodbye to an iconic platform. It was at AFS Chandigarh that the MiG-21 was inducted into the IAF with 28 Squadron, the 'First Supersonics', in 1963.

Marking their final few moments with the IAF, seven MiG-21 Bisons, including a single-seater aircraft flown by Chief of the Air Staff, Air Chief Marshal AP Singh, were airborne. The aircraft participated in a flypast with Sepecat Jaguar strike fighters, followed by a joint flypast with the Tejas light fighter that is replacing the MiG-21 in IAF service. On their return, a ceremonial water cannon salute and the final engine switch-off of the Bisons in front of various dignitaries drew the type's operational service with the IAF to an end.

Speaking following the retirement of the type, India's Defence Minister Rajnath Singh said: "In every historic mission, the MiG-21 carried the Tricolour with honour. Its contribution has never been limited to a single event or battle, it has been a pillar of India's air power for decades."

MiG-21s in the IAF

The IAF principally operated three major variants of the MiG-21. The MiG-21FL 'Trishul' (Type-77) was inducted between 1966-74, followed by the MiG-21M 'Badal' (Type-96) between 1973-81 and the MiG-21bis 'Vikram'

A pair of IAF MiG-21 Bisons stand silent following the culmination of the type's service with the IAF in September. In total, the IAF operated six squadrons of the type, along with some examples flying with the Tactics and Air Combat Development Establishment (TACDE)

Three IAF MiG-21 Bisons receive a final water canon salute at AFS Chandigarh on their return from a formation flypast, prior to their retirement from service on September 26 Images Zone Victor, unless stated

The MiG-21 Bison Document Form-700 being handed over to the Chief of the Air Staff, Air Chief Marshal AP Singh by the commanding officer of 23 Squadron. India's Defence Minister Rajnath Singh (second to right) is standing with Air Marshal Jeetendra Mishra, Air Officer Commanding-in-Chief Western Air Command next to him *Indian MoD*

Above: The six pilots tasked with flying the last sorties of the MiG-21 in IAF service are pictured here, including the commanding officer of 23 Squadron 'Panthers' (third from left). Air Chief Marshal AP Singh also joined the formation, flying a MiG-21 Bison single-seater (callsign 'Badal 3') Indian MoD

(Type-75) that was inducted between 1978-87. A few examples of the MiG-21PF (Type 76) were inducted earlier in March 1965 and, later that year, the air force received its first MiG-21U (Type 66) tandem-seat trainers.

HAL began assembly of the MiG-21FL in 1966, eventually producing a total of 205. Induction of the more versatile MiG-21M began towards the end of the 1960s, with 48 aircraft imported directly from the Soviet Union. Licence production of this variant began in India in 1973 with the last of 158 aircraft delivered in 1981.

India chose to retain the same engine for the MiG-21FL and the MiG-21M in the Tumansky R-11 turbojet, compared with the uprated R-13 of the MF variant. The IAF did evaluate two MiG-21M aircraft, one fitted with the R-13 and another with the R-11. However, over the course of evaluations between 1973-75, it was found the R-13 did indeed provide a noticeable improvement in performance at low and medium altitudes – but, the R-11 was selected as the engine was already being produced under licence in India by HAL.

The MiG-21bis powered by the R-25-300 engine was the final Russian evolution of the delta-winged fighter. The more powerful R-25 delivered 4,100kg of max dry thrust and 6,850kg of thrust in maximum reheat; 75 aircraft were imported directly from the Soviet Union and at its peak, ten IAF squadrons were equipped with the MiG-21bis. These aircraft had an airframe life of only 1,200 hours with major overhauls due at 600 hours.

The bis variant was armed with the GSh 23mm cannon and could carry four 250kg or two 500kg dumb bombs. Air-to-air armament initially comprised R3S IR-homing missiles or R3R radar-guided missiles, with French Magic-I IR homing missiles being integrated later. Two UB-32 rocket pods could be carried on the inner pylons along with two UB-16 rocket pods on the outer pylons.

The last of the IAF's long-serving MiG-21FLs were phased out in December 2013, when four examples belonging to the Kalaikunda-based Operational Conversion Unit (OCU) in West Bengal were retired from service. At that time, approximately 80% of the IAF's fighter aircrews had flown the MiG 21FL and 90% had flown at least one variant of the MiG 21 at some stage in their flying careers.

A pair of MiG-21 Bisons take to the air for the final time with the Indian Air Force on September 26 at AFS Chandigarh. The type's retirement marks the end of the IAF's long association with the Russian delta-winged fighter that spanned 62 years, with more than 870 aircraft acquired Indian MoD

Above: A galaxy of the Indian military's serving top brass were present for the retirement of the MiG-21 from IAF service. Flanked on either side by the six pilots who flew the Bison on its retirement are, from left to right: Air Marshal Jeetendra Mishra Air AOC-in-C, Western Air Command; Chief of the Army Staff General Upendra Dwivedi; Chief of the Air Staff Air Chief Marshal AP Singh; Defence Minister Rajnath Singh; Chief of Defence Staff General Anil Chauhan; Chief of the Naval Staff Admiral Dinesh K Tripathi; and Vice-Chief of the Air Staff Air Marshal Narmdeshwar Tiwari Indian MoD

The last MiG-21M was phased out in December 2017, with the bis variants following soon after. In October 2023 – when 4 Squadron 'Oorials', which had continuously operated different variants of the MiG-21s since 1966, converted from the Bison to the Su-30MKI – the IAF was left with only two squadrons of the type.

Bison to the fore

The MiG-21bis was the most formidable variant of the diminutive delta-winged fighter operated by the IAF. Inducted into the IAF in 1978, it

Generations of IAF pilots and maintenance crew trained and honed their skills on the MiG-21 and pictured here are the next generation of the air force delivering a hearty farewell to their long-serving mount

A MiG-21 Bison after retirement with its air-to-air armament in the (left) Vympel R-73E (NATO name: AA-11 Archer), (middle) RVV-AE Vympel R-77 (AA-12 Adder) BVRAAM and (right) UB-16 rocket pods

An IAF MiG-21U Mongol twin-seat trainer is pictured following the type's retirement from service. The IAF did not upgrade any of its MiG-21 trainers to Bison standard

later that year. The upgrade at that time was estimated at US$570 million, but eventually grew to $626m. MiG-MAPO (Moscow Aircraft Production Organisation) touted that the upgrade would convert the second-generation fighter aircraft to a fourth-gen one. A tall claim indeed!

The IAF decided to upgrade 125 MiG-21bis aircraft to the MiG-21UPG 'Bison' ('son of Bis') standard, which would include two prototype aircraft (C 2777 and C 2769) for modification and flight testing. The upgraded aircraft duly received the serial CU 2777 and CU 2769, respectively.

The Bison received a new multi-mode pulse-doppler radar in the Phazotron Kopyo-I (Spear), Ring Laser-based Inertial Navigation System (INS), Global Positioning System (GPS), indigenously developed Tarang Radar Warning Receiver (RWR), Counter Measure Dispensing System (CMDS), Self Protection Jammer (SPJ) pod and new air-to-air and air-to-ground weapons (KAB-500 TV guided bomb). As an interesting aside, the Russians charged India US$840,000 per Kopyo radar, which was a smaller version of the Zhuk-ME radar on the MiG-29.

The indigenous 'Tarang' RWRs were developed by the Defence Avionic and Research Establishment (DARE) in Bangalore and produced by Bharat Electronics Limited (BEL) Bengaluru. The most important upgrade to the type's aerial weaponry was the integration of the Vympel R-73E (AA-11 Archer) close-combat missile (CCM) and Vympel R-77/RVV-AEE (AA-12 Adder) BVR air-

was licence-manufactured by HAL with 220 produced by 1987, with the IAF operating 210 of these aircraft by 1995.

The MiG-21UPG initiative was aiming to deliver an air defence fighter with limited ground-attack capability. The IAF was eyeing an upgrade of its MiG-21bis fleet and, following the collapse of the Soviet Union in late 1991, the Russian Federation proposed an upgrade to the type in 1992. This was approved by the government of India in January 1996 with a formal contract inked

IAF MIG-21 Bisons were upgraded primarily to enhance their interception capability. However, the type had a more than useful secondary ground attack capability, as evidenced by the range of weapons and ammunition displayed here

Pictured, the initial batch of Indian pilots who ferried the first MiG-21F-13s (Type-74) to India Author collection

to-air missiles. The first of the RVV-AEs was delivered to the IAF in 2002 and the missiles had a shelf-life of eight years.

Cockpit display upgrades included a head-up-display (HUD), multi-function display (MFD) and helmet-mounted sighting device (HMSD). The hands-on-throttle and stick (HOTAS) concept was also incorporated, as was a video recording system (VRS). Externally, the biggest change was the incorporation of a single-piece front windshield and an HMSD compatible canopy. Several indigenous avionics systems were integrated, too. The Total Calendar Life / Total Technical Life of the upgraded aircraft was extended to 40 years as part of the upgrade, in addition to airframe modifications for carriage of SPJ pods.

The first Russian-modified MiG-21 Bison made its maiden flight from Nizhny Novgorod on October 1, 1998, though the official first flight was conducted on October 3. Hindustan Aeronautics was to have completed the modification of all aircraft at its Nasik Division by September 2001.

No. 3 Squadron was the first to induct the MiG-21 Bison and the last of an eventual 123 upgraded aircraft was delivered by HAL to the IAF in 2008. In total, the MiG-21 Bison operated with six IAF squadrons, in addition to being flown by the Gwalior-based Tactical and Combat Development and Training Establishment (TACDE). All maintenance activities relating to I and II line servicing of Bison aircraft were carried out at operating bases, with III and IV line servicing by HAL Nasik. Interestingly, while HAL has long since ceased production of MiG fighters in India, it continues to manufacture and overhaul Sukhoi SU-30MKIs at its facility which is still named the 'MiG Complex' in Nasik!

Force multiplier

In total, 27 IAF squadrons/establishments were equipped with the MiG-21 with the type showcasing its combat prowess in the 1971 war with Pakistan, with four Pakistani F-104s, two F-6s, one F-86 Sabre and a Lockheed C-130 Hercules downed. The pin-point rocket strikes by MiG-21s on the Governor's House at Dhaka also proved to be a turning point in the war. Decades later, MiG-21s were pressed into service during the 1999 Kargil War and again during Operation Balakot in 2019 and most recently during Operation Sindoor, earlier this year. It is perhaps fitting that the MiG-21 was on the front line again, even as its decades of service came to an end.

For the IAF, its MiG-21 variants allowed it to grow into a powerful air arm, while the final 'Bison' variant enabled it to retain its combat squadron strength. There is no doubt that the MiG-21 leaves behind a tremendous legacy within the IAF, even though its public image has been tarnished by questions about the type's accident rate, resulting in unsavoury nicknames such as 'flying coffin'.

As a fighter designed in the 1950s, with the definitive MiG-21bis ready in the 1970s, the aircraft was difficult to fly, just like many others of its era, such as the F-104 Starfighter. Speaking at a seminar following the type's retirement, former air force chief, Air Chief Marshal BS Dhanoa said that across 15,84,522 total service flying hours with the IAF, the MiG-21 had 468 accidents. Its accident rate of 2.95 matched that of the swing-wing MiG-23 (2.95) and was similar to MiG-27 (3.04), but much lower than the Hawker Hunter (4.26) and Folland Gnat (6.88).

The retirement of the MiG-21 fleet leaves the IAF with only 29 fighter squadrons. The IAF anticipated the retirement of 12 squadrons of MiG-21s and MiG-27s in ten years, a situation that has now come to pass with no early replacements in sight. The delays in the Tejas programme over the decades forced the IAF to retain its MiG-21s far longer than originally envisaged. As an example, the MiG-21 Bison fleet was initially scheduled for retirement in 2017, a story not too dissimilar from Poland's Su-22 *Fitter* (see *A Fitting Farewell*, page 28-33).

The IAF now has 180 indigenously developed Tejas Mk-1A fighter aircraft on order from HAL, a type that is far more than a 'like-for-like' replacement for the MiG-21 Bison and a truly multi-role platform. The air force has also made its preference clear for the procurement of 114 additional Dassault Rafale fighter jets. As a result, nearly 300 modern fighter jets will be inducted into the IAF over the next ten to 15 years, with other new inductions also planned.

The MiG-21 was often the first choice for IAF commanders as it provided unmatched flexibility due to its unique attributes of high agility, fast acceleration and quick turn-around. It is to the credit to the IAF and HAL that the aircraft remained relevant and supportable as long as it did. Even its final few weeks in service, IAF MiG-21 Bisons were flying extensively, as observed by the author. In the final analysis, it was the MiG-21 that built the foundations of the modern Indian Air Force, as we know it today and its legacy will be taken forward by another single-engine fighter type, the indigenously-built Tejas Mk-1A. **afm**

The precision rocket attacks carried out by the 'First Supersonics' with their MiG-21s is evident in this image of Tejgaon airfield (now in Bangladesh) during the 1971 war Author collection

New tricks for
old dogs

Exercise Anatolian Eagle took place at Konya Air Base, Turkey recently. While there, **Alan Warnes** discovered lessons learnt from Ukraine and Middle East conflicts were being implemented, with a focus on drones and ballistic missiles

There aren't too many European exercises where you get Arab air forces mixing in with those from NATO, but that's just what Exercise Anatolian Eagle (AE) has regularly been serving up since 2001.

After last year's hiatus due to runway work, Konya Air Base (3rd Main Jet Base) in central Turkey was back in business again. Base personnel claim it is one of only four tactical training centres in the world, the other three being CFB Cold Lake, Canada (Maple Flag),

Nellis AFB, USA (Red Flag) and the Aerospace Centre of Excellence (ACE) at PAF Base Mushaf, Pakistan. However, it doesn't include, not too surprisingly, the Air Tactics Center at Andravida, Greece, which hosts Exercise Iniochos every year.

This year's edition, which took place between June 23 and July 3, involved realistic, high-end combat scenarios designed to refine tactics, address advanced threats and develop combat-credible forces.

Enter the drones

AE exercises have in recent years provided the Turkish defence industry an opportunity to show their products on an international stage. AE25 was different, new Turkish systems were incluuded in new tactical scenarios, like counter-ballistic missile ops and manned-unmanned teaming.

The Konya Base Commander, General Mete Kuş told reporters that this year's AE provided "high, realistic, multinational

A Royal Saudi Air Force Boeing F-15SA Eagle taxies out for a SEAD mission past the Qatar Emiri Air Force Typhoons
All photos, Alan Warnes unless stated

A Boeing E-7T AEW&C of 131 Filo 'Edjerler' taxies down the Konya runway during the elephant walk. The Turkish Air Force operates four of these, all based at Konya, which are a regular feature of Anatolian Eagle, they provide the situational awareness of the air war

training environments to align partner air forces with its continuously improving infrastructure and technological capabilities".

One new approach compared to previous occasions which separates it from most international exercises, was the participation of unmanned aerial vehicle systems (UAVs) or drones.

They were all indigenous platforms, the stealthy looking TAI Anka-III UCAV, along with the company's Aksungur and Anka-S, as well as the Bayraktar Akinci all played a part. Unfortunately, an Anka III crashed in the early stages of the exercise, but it's thought to have been replaced.

Exercise Director Major Ekrem Cekin spoke more about the drones: "For the first time in an internationally conducted exercise within the scope of conventional operations, UAVs have been assigned direct strike missions. More importantly, manned fighter aircraft conducted escort and protection missions for them."

Many air forces and defence companies are now bidding to integrate UAVs with manned fighters in what is termed MUM-T or crewed-uncrewed teaming (CUC-T) to increase combat mass, at a fraction of the cost of buying and operating all manned fighters. Turkey's Turkish Aerospace Industries is among the companies leading the way in the international arena, pairing UAVs with the future Kaan fifth-generation fighter."

Cekin stated: "This represents one of the most advanced examples of manned-unmanned systems integration and showcases the technology-driven capabilities of the Turkish armed forces and Turkish industry."

These developments, he said, would not only reflect the scope of the exercise but a vision for an air force, that is preparing for the operational environments of the future.

He added: "Anatolian Eagle is a product of joint training, shared understanding and collective deterrence."

Unfortunately, we didn't get the opportunity to see the drones or find out more on how the TurAF [Turkish Air Force] was approaching this.

While we were told the drones were used in a strike role, there is some speculation that some may have been used as part of the IHASOJ (İnsansız Hava Aracı Stand-Off-Jammer) project, aimed at using UAV platforms, like the Bayraktar Akinci, in the electronic warfare roles.

They will become part of an EW system the TurAF is currently evolving, with four new Global 6000 HAVA SOJ electronic attack aircraft. HAVA SOJ is being managed by a joint Aselsan/TAI project team, ordered in 2018 that should now see the first aircraft delivered next year, with all four delivered by 2028. Four new hangars are being built at Konya to house them, located close to the Boeing E-7T Peace Eagle Airborne Early Warning and Control (AEW&C) facility.

Cekin confirmed the land-based EW KARASOJ system was being used at AE, designed to search, intercept, analyse, classify

Above: This weathered looking Royal Jordanian Air Force F-16BM, with a newly painted Have Glass-style tail taxies out for another mission. This was one of three Jordanian F-16s, with the other two being single-seaters. It previously served the Royal Netherlands Air Force as J-270.

Below: The pilot of this F-16CM flown by the 510th Fighter Squadron keeps the jet low after take-off. Stencilled along the side are 27 of what look like drone kills it was accredited with during the unit's 209-day deployment to the Middle East which commenced on April 23 and ended on November 18 last year

International Participants 2025

Country/Org	Deployed aircraft	Mission
Azerbaijan	2 x Su-25	Air to ground
Hungary	3 x Gripen C/D	Air to Air
Qatar	3 x Typhoons	Multi-role
Jordan	3 x F-16AM/BM	Multi-role
Saudi	6 x F-15SA/SR	SEAD/Multi-role
US	12 x F-16CM/DM	Multi-role
NATO	1 x E-3A	C2
No of aircraft	30	

All six Royal Saudi Air Force F-15SA/SRs lined up on the ramp after flying had completed on July 3. The big twin-engine jets fulfilled the SEAD mission and were equipped with Sniper targeting pods

Turkish participants

Unit	Deployed aircraft	Mission
113 Filo 'Ceylan'	4 x F-16C	Multi-role
131 Filo 'Edjerler'	3 x E-7T	Multi-role
132 Filo 'Hanceler'	10 x F-16C/D	Multi-role inc
		Red Air
135 Filo 'Ates'	1 x CN235	Airlift
151 Filo 'Tunc'	5 x F-16C	SEAD/Multi role
152 Filo 'Akinci'	5 x F-16C	Multi-role
161 Filo 'Kartel'	3 x F-16C	Multi-role
162 Filo 'Zipkin'	3 x F-16C	Multi-role
191 Filo 'Kobra'	3 x F-16C	Multi-role
101 Filo 'Asenalar'	1 x KC-135R	AAR
311 Filo	2 x Anka-S/Akinci	A/G ISR
TAI	1 x Anka 3	A/G
	1 x Aksungur	A/G ISR
No of aircraft	42	

There were three F-16Cs from 191 Filo 'Kobra', based at Balikeshir, at AE25 fulfilling the multirole mission, like most Turkish F-16 units. Oddly this jet was equipped with two indigenous SDT ACMI pods

Above: A specially marked Turkish Air Force/151 Filo F-16C from Merzifon in northern Turkey. For its suppression of enemy air defence role it is equipped with the AGM-88 heat-seeking anti-radiation missile (HARM). There were five 151 Filo F-16s present

Right: A 193 Filo F-16D from Balikeshir departs Konya. The jet must have been used by another unit, as 193 Filo was not present at AE25

Below: Two Qatar Emiri Air Force Eurofighter Typhoons taxi back to their parking spot after a mission on July 3. Both were fitted with Cubic ACMI pods and IRST training missiles

and locate the directions of enemy radar signals, then jam, deceive or disrupt the radars. Unfortunately, no more detail was provided.

He added that this year's training included for the first time ever the interception of cruise missiles, emphasising early detection, identification and then neutralisation.

Cruise missiles with low radar cross sections, simulated by TAI Super Simsek and Simsek target drones were fired from Anka III UCAVs that we were told were engaged through joint missions, involving airborne and ground-based systems.

Blue Force elements conducted interception and elimination operations in response to the simulated cruise missile attacks launched by the Red Force. This scenario tested the joint reaction capabilities of the TurAF and allied units against asymmetric missile threats

To suppress threats, complex missions

This beautiful looking Azerbaijan Su-25 departs for a ground attack role. The two Frogfoots always departed last, as they could only stay airborne for about 30 minutes

Clearly the TurAF, like so many other air forces, is learning lessons from the war in Ukraine. We all recall that, in early 2022, the Ukrainian leadership would not believe the Russians would attack. Well, for the first time in an international exercise, crisis phase scenarios preceding the outbreak of war were simulated through actual flight missions. Within this framework, pilots were trained in preventative air operation planning, and rules of engagement and deterrence techniques aimed at preventing a surprise attack before conflict erupts.

AE25 also saw Turkish SDT (Space and Defence Technologies) marketing its ACMI (Air Combat Manoeuvring Instrumentation) pods that had replaced the more familiar Cubic ACMI pods on Turkish Air Force and Royal Jordanian Air Force F-16s.

were conducted that included maritime assets, with four Turkish Navy vessels TCG *Akar*, TCG *Bafra*, TCG *Gediz* and TCG *Zipkin* involved, while operating in the Aegean Sea, along with integrated air-to-air and air-to-ground missions. These operations tested the capabilities of not just pilots, but also mission planners, command and control staff, and ground support teams.

It is understandable that the latest developments in the aggressive use of cruise and ballistic missiles, witnessed during the Ukraine/Russia and Iran/Israel conflicts were introduced into AE and will surely be implemented in every other half-decent exercise. Introducing the latest threats into such an exercise was a bold move by the Anatolian Eagle planners, and hopefully in Anatolian Eagle 26 they might reveal more.

This F-16CM sports the dark grey Have Glass colour scheme that is now becoming increasingly common in the USAF F-16 fleet. The new paint job is meant to reduce the jet's radar signature

Two Hungarian Air Force Gripen Cs taxi back to their parking spot after completing a combat air patrol mission

A clean-looking F-16C from 113 Filo 'Ceylan' ('Gazelle') normally based at Eskisehir departs for another mission

The Weapons Systems Officer of this 132 Filo F-16D excitedly waves his Turkish flag in the rear seat. On the centre station under the jet you can see an AN/ALQ-131 ECM (Electronic Counter Measures) pod used to jam the systems of the Blue Air aircraft

According to a company spokesperson, they can be integrated on both western and eastern airborne platforms. He also said the system has a range of up to 100 miles in the air-to-air configuration and 200 miles in the air to ground.

Flying

Probably one of the most welcome visitors at AE25 was the 31st Fighter Wing's 510th Fighter Squadron 'Buzzards' which brought 12 F-16CMs/DMs from Aviano Air Base, Italy. For seven months last year, while on a Central Command deployment to the Middle East, the unit flew a whopping 8,800 hours and 1,400 sorties. Judging from the large number of mission marks worn by several of the F-16s at AE25, they were kept very busy! Some were defensive counter air missions to protect US Naval assets travelling through the Bab el Mandeb Strait in the Persian Gulf (for more see News). No doubt they would have passed some of what they learnt onto allies, even if much of the team on that deployment has probably moved on.

By July 2, the 510th had flown 88 sorties out of 111 planned missions over the two weeks, so missing out on 23 which was not too surprising, considering the jets are around 35 years old and been well used over the intervening years. The unit

was trying, ambitiously, to fly between six and eight F-16s in each of the two waves every day which must have kept their maintenance personnel extremely busy. The only squadron to fly anywhere near their numbers, was 132 Filo the TurAF aggressor squadron, which was also flying FY88/89 F-16s but without the number of hours that have been clocked on their airframes. They

had flown 85 out of a planned 87 by July 2.

Exercise Anatolian Eagle is a big attraction for Arab air forces, and this year was no different, with Jordanian F-16AM/BMs, Qatari Typhoons and Saudi F-15SA/SR Eagles all present flying multi-role missions, although the Royal Saudi Air Force Eagles also flew Suppression of Enemy Air Defence (SEAD) sorties.

These two Azerbaijan Air Force Su-25 Frogfoots depart on another ground attack mission. The contrasting colour schemes illustrate the difference between the upgraded and non-upgraded aircraft

The elephant walk organised this year for the first time in several years, was witnessed by around 1,000 'spotters' on July 2 Cem Dogut

Exercise Report: Anatolian Eagle 25

Getting the opportunity to work with NATO and vice-versa, to learn from each other in the biggest tactical training range in Europe is a big factor in their appearances at Konya. This was, according to the Hungarian Air Force which was making its debut at an Anatolian Eagle exercise, the reason they were there.

The Royal Saudi Air Force (RSAF) brought four F-15SAs and two F-15SR Eagles from 92 Squadron at Dhahran which are a much more sophisticated version of the USAF F-15E Strike Eagle. As a bit of background, the RSAF took delivery of 84 F-15SAs between 2017-2022 which are now being upgraded and 72 F-15S between 1996-99, 64 of the latter have been upgraded to F-15SR by Al Salam Aircraft Industries (now SAMI) at its Riyadh site. There is no external difference between the F-15SA and F-15SR.

*Above: **This beautifully marked F-4E Phantom, 77-0303, was painted in these special markings to celebrate the legendary jet's 50th anniversary serving the TurAF last year. It didn't play any part in the exercise other than head up the elephant walk and perform a flying routine for the media and spotters***

*Left: **A dual-seat F-16D of the Aviano-based 510th Fighter Squadron taxies out for another mission. Taking two-seaters to these exercises allows senior officers or less experienced aviators a chance of seeing the action in the air up close***

*Below: **It isn't all about fighters at Anatolian Eagle, the based 135 Filo used a CN 235 to undertake airlift missions***

were fitted with Belarussian Talisman electronic warfare pods to jam enemy radar signals.

The Hungarian Air Force Gripens were quite a surprise, given they had never attended before and were set to start a Baltic Air Policing commitment less than a month later, on August 1. They flew on most days on combat air patrols, although during the author's two-day stay the dual seater never flew.

The other Middle East attendees were three Royal Jordanian Air Force F-16s, comprising two single-seat F-16AMs and a fab-looking dual-seat F-16BM wearing USAF type serial (see page 50). They flew two aircraft on each wave that usually included the two-seater, so making the most of their time there. The three Qatar Emir Air Force Eurofighter Typhoons also flew two aircraft on each wave, but all were single seaters.

By the end of the two weeks of drills, Qatar had flown 23 missions, Jordan 16 and Saudi Arabia 50, providing pilots with invaluable experience to take back home.

Other exotic visitors included two Azerbaijan Air Force Su-25 *Frogfoots*. One (Bort No 27 white) was sporting a brand-new grey colour scheme it received after being upgraded under the Laçin Modernisation Programme and now re-designated a Su-25ML. The first conversion was delivered in July 2023 and involves the integration of new Turkish munitions that included the Teber-82 laser guided bombs, KGK-82 and KGK-83 glide bombs, and the SOM-B1 stand-off weapon. There is a second stage that involves a comprehensive avionics upgrade supported through the Aselsan Advanced Modular Computer and LGK-82/83 laser guided bombs and the SOM Sahin, a spin-off of the SOM. The two aircraft at AE25

The Anka III comes into land minus the Simshek or Super Simsek drones under its wings. They were used as ballistic missiles during the drills that would be attacked by fighters. A new scenario in exercises that have been played out for real in both Ukraine and the Middle East Cem Doghut

The Egyptian Air Force had been expected to send three F-16s but unfortunately cancelled at the last minute, while the Pakistan Air Force was going to send six JF-17C Block 3s but backed out after the outbreak of war in neighbouring Iran.

Mission

On the July 3 Eagle COMAO (composite air operation) witnessed by the author, the first aircraft to depart at 0830hrs was a NATO E-3 AWACS, which would have been involved in the supervision of Blue Air fighters. It was followed by an AEW&C E-7T Peace Eagle,

Modern Turkish indigenous UAVs involved at AE25 – the Anka III on the left has two Simshek/Super Simshek high speed drones under the wings. These would have been used to mimic ballistic missiles during AE25

that might have been assisting the Red Air or alternatively flying on a TurAF mission.

The first fighters to leave were two Saudi F-15SAs that departed at 0859hrs. Half an hour later two Royal Saudi Air Force F-15SA/SRs and four 510th FS F-16CMs of the 30 international participants departed, their mission was to stop the Red Air ground based air defences from 'shooting down' the Blue Air participants that followed including the Azerbaijan Air Force Su-25s, Hungarian Gripens, Qatari Typhoons and Jordanian F-16s. Turkish Air Force F-16s from various units joined them, while 132 Filo sent up ten F-16C/Ds as the Red Air force to mix it up. The last fighter took off at 1024hrs and returned by 1215hrs.

The bulk of the 30 international participants flying alongside 38 TurAF assets was made up of 33 F-16s, three E-7T AEW&C aircraft, one CN 235 transport aircraft and a KC-135 tanker was enough to ensure a good fight.

While there were just seven different TurAF F-16 squadrons present, other F-16s were evident, from the likes of 191 and 193 Filo from Balikesir, and 181 Filo from Diyarbakir.

AE25 was once again a great spectacle and the TurAF even organised an elephant walk, representing the different units that were involved. Unfortunately, a drone was not involved and clearly the TurAF isn't confident enough to show these off yet or even talk about them in any detail, so let's hope they go one step further next year. After all, if you are willing to talk about the capability, then why not show it off too? **afm**

KEY
Publishing

Understanding the Rafale kills

Alan Warnes gained rare and exclusive access to the Pakistan Air Force in mid-July, to understand how it managed to shoot down six Indian Air Force fighters on the night of May 6/7

With vapour streaming from its wing tips, this camouflaged Chengdu J-10C looks every inch the deadly fighter it was on May 6/7 All images Alan Warnes unless stated

PAF Commander, ACM Zaher Ahmed Baber Sidhu has revolutionised the PAF over the past four years. PAF

"**W**e ambushed them," a high-ranking PAF officer told me in mid-July. "We trapped them in our kill chain and created chaos."

That's how the PAF claims it shot down six Indian Air Force (IAF) fighters in the early hours of May 7, when the biggest beyond visual range (BVR) air battle was contested on Pakistan's border with India.

The IAF had launched Operation Sindoor (Sindoor being an orange/red powder worn by Hindu women). The PAF retaliated with a counter-operation, Operation Bunyan-un-Marsoos, (an Arabic phrase meaning a solid structure, derived from the Quran.)

More than 114 fighters were involved - 72 IAF and 42 from the PAF - most believed to be fitted with BVR missiles developed by the French, Israelis, Russians and Chinese.

The senior officer said: "Fifty-two minutes after the air war had started, the fight was over, we won and they headed home.

"We could have shot down more Rafales than we did, but we held back. An escalation could have led to all-out war between two nuclear nations. During Op Bunyan-un-Marsoos we targeted the Rafales and the S-400s [Russian air defence system] and it worked out well!"

Unfolding air war

India had been seeking revenge for the Pahalgam terror attack that took place in Indian-administered Kashmir on April 22, when five armed terrorists killed 26 mainly Hindu civilians. India's government, led by Prime Minister Narendra Modi, blamed Pakistan for this atrocity and he, along with the majority of the Indian public seemingly, wanted revenge.

"We watched while on full alert, waiting for a response," the PAF officer told me. For six tense days, the PAF monitored the build-up of transport aircraft, supporting large deployments of fighters to several IAF Western Command and South-Western Command bases. They knew an attack was imminent and were prepared for it.

Each of the four Air Commands – North, Central, South and West – operates deployable command and control (C2) centres, capable of directing operations across vast distances. Among their many functions one stood out for the author - the long-range vectoring of hypersonic missiles, like the CM-400AKGs that the PAF JF-17C Thunder jets launched at some of the most formidable assets in India's arsenal. They included the highly advanced Russian-built S-400 air defence systems (see *The S-400 Quandary*, pages 38-41).

The author was granted rare access to one of the deployable C2 centres, witnessing first-hand how it functioned. It is part of the PAF

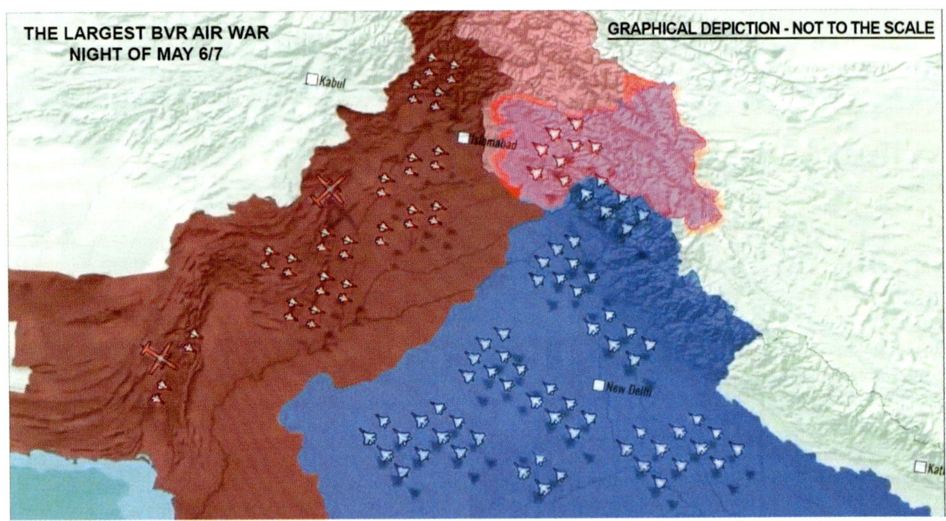

On May 6/7 the two air forces faced off, looking across their borders in formations like this PAF

The PAF Commander's inner circle in the wake of the air battle with the IAF on May 7. This is the Multi Domain Ops room, where all the data was fed in from different sensors PAF

The PAF Commander, ACM Zaheer Ahmed Baber Sidhu in the National ISR and Integrated Air Ops Center (NIIACC) during Op Bunyan-un-Marsoos PAF

PAF's Link 17 (and the enhanced Skyguard system), fed to the JF-17s, J-10Cs and Erieye to provide pilots with the situational awareness needed to win a war.

This means every cockpit receives a Recognised Air Picture through encrypted datalinks, ensuring PAF aircrew possess the tactical clarity needed to dominate the skies. This fusion of space, cyber, electronic warfare (EW) and kinetic power has turned the PAF into a truly multi-domain combat force, capable of deterring, responding and prevailing in future wars, which seems highly likely. This capability has been built up since the author's last visit in 2020 and was clearly revolutionising the way PAF the trains and goes to war.

Several military veterans the author spoke to were keen to stress that the PAF is just part of the fighting machine run by the Chief of Army Staff, Field Marshal Asim Munir who made a high-profile visit to the USA in mid-August. He harnesses the combined strengths of Army, Navy and Air Force, but this feature focusses on the PAF.

EW at work

On April 29, a week after the Pahalgam attack, four IAF Rafales departed Ambala Air Force Station. Their mission, to bomb terrorist targets in the north, but according to the PAF, a mobile PAF electronic warfare (EW) unit deployed

Chief of the Air Staff, Air Chief Marshal Zaheer Ahmed Baber Sidhu's integrated multi-domain operations philosophy he has pursued since becoming PAF Commander in March 2021 – for more on that see later. An Air Vice Marshal from the newly created Space Force added: "The C2 centres are reliable and robust and can see across the border into India, but I won't disclose the range due to the sensitive nature. Fusing data with our new unmanned, space, EW and cyber commands means they are effectively our nerve centres."

PAF's Space Command has redefined the battlespace. Using indigenous satellites, it delivers round-the-clock intelligence, surveillance and reconnaissance (ISR) support. The Global Navigation Satellite System (GNSS), datalinks real-time information to PAF aircraft bypassing the limitations of the line-of-sight communication. Through secure SATCOM connectivity, pilots not only gain unmatched situational awareness but also offensive capabilities like electronic attack. It's a central piece of the

All new air doctrine is created and tested at the PAF's ACE facility, based at Mushaf, that has a huge tactical training range - one of the best in the world according to the Turkish Air Force (see last month's Anatolian Eagle exercise report)

The PAF operates 20 J-10C Vigorous Dragons in both camouflaged and grey markings. None currently wear squadron markings but that could change soon. This aircraft, with its light blue underbelly, taxies to the end of the Minhas runway for a mission

A grey J-10C with six hard-points under the wings, two equipped with twin missile racks. During the author's time at Minhas, a grey example always flew with a camouflaged jet

by the power output, and a lack of this power will make the jammer less effective at disrupting intended signals. This would have been the case with the S-400 air defence system or Rafale's Thales RBE2 radar, which MBDA designed to be robust against jamming, and integrated with the passive Thales Spectra EW system.

The EW mobile units designed by the new NASTP (National Aerospace Science & Technology Park) in recent years, instigated by the PAF's Commander, ACM Sidhu, were being fielded at various locations to jam targets. Between April 29, when the IAF tried their failed attack, and May 6, the PAF had watched the IAF deploy up to 20 Rafales from Hashimara (home of 101 Sqn in the Eastern Command) to Gwalior and several other bases (Ambala, home of 17 Sqn Rafales in Western Command, Srinagar and Bikaner/Nal in Rajasthan). Several S-400 *SA-21 Growler* surface-to-air missile batteries were moved to Adampur, Bhuj and Bikaner.

The IAF mobilised around 400 aircraft in late April and early May, with the transport fleet flying over 500 sorties, obviously to move around weapons, logistics and personnel for an attack. The PAF was prepared.

along the front line saw them approaching and jammed their radars and communications, while cyber-attacks on electric grids in the north, rendered the Rafales helpless. They abandoned their mission and instead diverted to Srinagar Air Force Station.

The Dassault 20ECMs of 24 'Blinders' Squadron which had performed so well in Op Swift Retort in February 2019 (see panel) were not used in Operation Bunyan-un-Marsoos because of their lack in wattage power. Trying to overpower a target receiver is heavily influenced

Three J-10C flying line abreast armed with 18 air-to-air missiles between them. The Chinese People's Liberation Army Air Force is now keen to understand how the PAF worked their jets so well operationally

"We could not let the attack go unpunished. No one infringes Pakistani sovereign territory, and we are entrusted to protect it."

ACM Sidhu has boosted the PAF's capabilities considerably with his operational and industry visions. He is seen here walking to a F-16 alongside members of his staff and base personnel PAF

Rafales, Su-30MKIs and Mirage 2000s."

Most of the IAF's 36 Rafales were flying in offensive mode on the Indian side of the border at some point and according to the PAF, they were equipped with MBDA's highly capable Meteor BVRAAM, backed up by Su-30MKI *Flankers* armed with Israeli Derby BVR missiles and Spice 2000 precision-guided munitions (PGMs).

According to the ISPR (Inter Services Public Relations) press briefing on May 7, the IAF had eight formations lined up along the eastern border, each strike package comprised eight aircraft: four Su-30MKIs, two Rafales and two Mirage 2000s.

Locking on the target

A senior PAF pilot explained how they prepare for war with India, always a real possibility. "It's in the training," he said. "Going to theatre, the fighter's radar cannot see all the targets as they are too far away, but the Saab 2000 Erieye does."

As a high value asset and undoubtedly a target for India, the Saab 2000 Erieye will keep out of harm's way flying close to the western border, over 400km (250 miles) from India.

He continued: "The operator sitting in front of his screen in the Erieye will label the enemy aircraft into the different groups and assign them to the PAF packages. This will be done in groups of three or four aircraft according to azimuth and altitude, then the operator assesses and relays [the positions] to all the aircraft, but he will still control them.

"The war picture is built through Link 17/Skyguard, which we see on the displays in our cockpit, and the aircraft we are assigned to shoot – which we term 'the contract'. The Air Boss and his team [in the Multi Domain Ops Room] will also be looking over the scene on a massive screen in AHQ.

"The fighter pilots have two radios in the cockpit, one to discuss the complete aerial picture and another to talk to members in your formation.

"If I am targeting their no 1 and 2, I would see them on my scope, put my cursor on them and lock my missiles onto them.

At 1230hrs on May 7, that attack came when the IAF bombed nine sites in Pakistan with long-range Spice 2000 precision-guided bombs. The CAS immediately changed the rules of engagement, with airborne PAF fighters instructed to move from defensive to offensive mode. He spoke directly to all the PAF pilots in the air via radio, commanding them to shoot them down, and according to several sources he told the airborne fighter pilots: "Kill them, kill them, don't let them enter even an inch into Pakistan."

The PAF could not let the attack go unpunished, and as the spokesman told me: "No one infringes Pakistani sovereign territory - we are entrusted to protect it.

"When the IAF released those bombs, there were already 72 IAF aircraft in the air, as their numbers had steadily increased. We started the attack on the different strike packages of

With its front wheel lifting off the runway, this J-10C is set for another mission

The Tactics Developments School is where the anti-Rafale ops are rolled out to PAF personnel. The PAF has always worked harder to define tactics against its Indian foe and no stone is left unturned to ensure that they are successful

"My radar is then locked onto the target and is linking info to the missile until a certain range, when the missile switches on to its own AESA [Active Electronically Scanned Array] seeker within the PL-15's minimum abort range [MAR]."

The MAR is the closest an engaging aircraft can get to the target and fire the missile before getting out of a fight, before the missile threat is able to run you down.

"Once your missile's active range (in this case the PL-15) is met, you can turn back (to ensure you don't fly inside the MAR of a Meteor -let's say 35 miles). The missile with its AESA seeker will then lock on to target and shoot it down."

The author was told the Rafale pilots would not have known what hit them until the PL-15Es were about three seconds out.

"Remember, if you miss your designated aircraft, it could get you. We train continuously for this. A mission of 15 minutes can regularly take up to eight hours to debrief!

"In a war theatre you can put as many aircraft as possible up. The IAF sent 72 into the AOR [Area of Responsibility] but it's a lot for the GCIs [Ground Control Interceptors] to control!"

One of the lessons the IAF must have learnt from that night was the sheer number of aircraft they deployed in the air was too much to handle. Each IAF GCI would have to manage several aircraft in an extremely dynamic situation, particularly as aircraft were being shot down. The PAF Commander said: "We designated an IAF aircraft for every J-10 or JF-17 Block 3 with the battle space being managed much better because of the multi domain ops."

Going for the kill

Waiting for the IAF fighters to make their move in the early hours of May 7 were PAF J-10C Vigorous Dragons and JF-17C

Preparing the PAF for Full Spectrum Air Ops, the Aerospace Power Centre of Excellence has all the elements of the PAF offensive force. The J-35 and ASOJ (Airborne Stand Off Jammer) are both listed. While ASOJ has been contracted with Turkey, the J-35 is still being studied

Thunders, both armed with Chinese PL-15s (CH-AA-10 *Abaddon*) BVRAAMs and shorter-range PL-10s (CH-AA-9 *Azrael*). Behind them were F-16C Block 52s with the shorter range AN/APG-68 radars, equipped with AIM-120C AMRAAMs (Advanced Medium Range Air to Air Missiles).

Highly capable and well-trained pilots from both sides were going into battle with an immense amount of national pride at stake.

As they raced towards each other and the missiles of the Indian fighters went 'hot', the PAF Commander gave the order from the NAIIOC (National ISR Air Ops Centre) to break their data links, which meant they would lose all situational awareness. Jamming from mobile EW units dotted all along the eastern fringes of Pakistan completed the damage.

The Rafale's cutting edge Thales Spectra integrated electronic warfare system was designed to protect the Indian Air Force's jet. The pilot should have been warned by Spectra that something was watching them, and they needed to start taking evasive action. Spectra should have detected the radar of the enemy aircraft's electromagnetic waves. Unless of course the J-10 did not switch on its radar, and the target information was data linked to the fighter that then fired the PL-15. When the missile eventually switched on its AESA seeker in the terminal phase, it would have been too late for the Rafale.

In the Ops room, the PAF Commander instructed a pilot to fire at their selected adversary, visible on the Comprehensive Complete Air Picture (CCAP) screen. The author was shown a recording of a PL-15E leaving the J-10's missile rail and tracking towards the red target. Once the target was hit, the signal would blink intermittently, until it disappeared. All the information on the targets was available to the PAF.

As one retired officer stated: "They were sitting ducks - they didn't stand a chance when our J-10Cs unleashed those PL-15s. Our Multi Domain Ops ensured the IAF pilots couldn't perform in the air battle."

The radar range of both the J-10C's KLJ-10 and the Rafale's RBE2 is believed to be around 200km (125 miles). According to the PAF, not one Meteor was fired at the PAF fighters. The PL-15Es hit their targets at between 160 and 190km (100 and 120 miles) out (close to the maximum kinetic range of the export version of PL-15), and with the Meteor's range only being about 150km, you can understand why. The PL-15E had an edge of about 40-50km and the IAF fighters were downed over Indian territory. The PL-15 is certainly faster than the Meteor so that would be another factor. The PAF effectively trapped the IAF pilots in their 'kill chain'.

Three of the IAF's satellites were by now under PAF control, using its indigenously developed systems. The downlinks were subsequently severed and the GPS signals were neutralised. At the same time, the PAF's cyber warriors

Indian Air Force losses

Indian Air Force losses
4 x Rafale EH
1 x Su-30MKI
1 x MiG-29UPG
1 x Mirage 2000H
1 x Heron Mk2

A J-10C sits on the edge of the 15 (Multi Role) Squadron shelter area, armed and looking very dangerous, Clearly visible is the IRST sensor on the nose and the air-to-air refuelling probe *PAF*

launched a sweeping offensive, crippling 96% of India's social networks, penetrating critical systems, and even disrupting the country's railways, airlines, banks and energy grids to sow chaos. Bold messages flashed across Indian CCTV screens, while websites were defaced and key digital nodes were struck, triggering electricity blackouts across vast regions of India. This was the first time any Air Force in the world had synced its cyber operations with its kinetic operations.

PAF Cyber Ops had shifted into offensive mode. Back in 2019 during Operation Swift Retort, there was no cyber footprint, but by 2021 work had commenced on creating the new command, which opened in May 2023 and started functioning in October 2024. PAF has created a cyber range, where cyber warfare skills are built up by pitching blue and red teams against each other. Elements of the PAF Cyber Force played an active role in achieving the right effects during Op Bunyan-un-Marsoos, when cyber was integrated with kinetic ops. PAF kept it all relevant by participating in operations and exercises like Indus Shield 24.

Breaking the news

News on this clash broke in Europe later that day (May 7) when the ISPR held a press conference.

The PAF's Deputy Chief of Air Staff (DCAS Operations) and Director General Public Relations (DGPR) took much of the world by surprise, when they claimed the PAF had shot down five IAF fighters. These included three, later increased to four, extremely capable 4.5-generation Rafales fitted with the cutting-edge Thales Spectra electronic warfare systems. The air-to-air kills were backed up by images from social media accounts and included GPS co-ordinates of where they crashed.

As the PAF's DCAS Ops disclosed at the press conference, attended by both local and international media, the IAF were continuously scrambling their fighters in the early hours, to reinforce and saturate the air defence. "Our strategy was to have force concentration in our selected AORs and fight to our own strength.

"Once they saw our numbers, the IAF fighters launched their ground weapons, and we identified them. As soon as this happened, the Chief changed the rules of engagement from 'deter' to 'sure kill'.

"We targeted the Rafales, because the IAF had always said they would make 'the difference'."

The DCAS (Ops) talked with the aid of a screen at the conference about the losses and the locations where they were shot down. The PAF had tapped into IAF Rafale communications, and listened to a four-ship 'Godzilla 1-4' formation in panic and distress, having discovered one of the French jets was missing.

He ran the recordings to assembled media, which was quite startling at the time, but it seems the Rafale pilots were mistakenly talking on an open frequency rather than a secure one. During the stand-off, the PAF identified 14 Rafales within the 72 aircraft, through its electronic intelligence systems, and then targeted them.

The PAF also struck the radar in the northern ICCS (Integrated Command and Control Centre) at Barnala which effectively stopped all communications between the IAF leadership and their fighters.

The Indian military fired Brahmos air/surface-to-ground missiles capable of speeds of 3,000km/h (1,900mph) one after the other. I was told by the PAF there had been 'soft kills' and 'hard kills' by the Brahmos. There is some suggestion the PAF jammed the Brahmos frequencies but no one would confirm this.

During the press briefing, the PAF spokesperson showed the radar signatures of the Brahmos on the screen, which he said missed targets and flew into Afghanistan.

After 52 minutes, the IAF fighters fled back to their bases, outwitted by the PAF. A senior officer, told the author: "The Rafale is potent

PL-15 amazes the world

The export version of the PL-15E was exhibited at Zhuhai in 2021 and again in 2024. The author was told the PAF's version had a range of around 190km (120 miles). The longest distance that any of the PAF missiles hit their target, was around 190km (120 miles). According to the International Institute of Strategic Studies (IISS) the PL-15 is known for its long-range capabilities and energetic boost-sustain motor. The 'boost-sustain' element is believed to refer to a two-stage motor, providing both initial acceleration and sustained flight. It makes it capable of speeds greater than Mach 5. After being fired and entering its terminal phase, the motor's second pulse will ignite, providing the additional thrust to increase kill probability at long distances. If the missile is launched at supersonic speed, as it would have been by the J-10Cs, it can maintain speeds of Mach 5+ for much of the flight. It will inevitably begin to slow down post motor burn out.

The PL-15/-15E is among a small number of AAMs that is guided by a miniature active electronically scanned array radar seeker that houses both active and passive modes. According to the IISS, Japan fields a BVR fitted with an AESA (AAM-4B) and there are suspicions that the US fields a AMRAAM version with an AESA that it doesn't export. According to the IISS, the missile features improved resistance to countermeasures and better performance against stealthy targets. It is also thought the hybrid guidance system supports a mini-course two-way datalink led by AEW&C aircraft.

The AEW&C can reportedly guide the missiles to their targets via Chinese XS-3 tactical data links, allowing them to be launched from a stand-off distance and "guided" to their respective targets... to remain undetected.

As a result, the PL-15E can be employed without relying on the onboard AESA radar for most of its flight, significantly reducing the likelihood of detection. The advantage of third-party targeting is in part that the launch aircraft may remain passive in the engagement.

The Saab 2000 Erieye was the unsung hero of Op Bunyan-un-Marsoos, supporting the situational requirements of the fighter packages

ripples of disbelief while addressing an Air Force Association gathering in Bangalore by saying: "We shot down five PAF fighters and an AEW&C Erieye with our S-400 SAMs at a range of 300 kilometres."

Coming three months after the battle had concluded, it not only contradicted the earlier admission by his superior, General Chauhan, but also lacked any supporting evidence.

It appeared to be a desperate attempt to placate Prime Minister Modi, whose government has been under mounting pressure to mask the scale of the IAF's losses. The stark contradiction between India's top military leaders underscores the turbulence within its defence establishment.

Training to fight Rafale

The IAF had bought 36 Dassault Rafales in 2016, along with MBDA Meteor BVRAAMs, MBDA Scalp EG/Storm Shadow cruise missiles and Safran AASM Hammer glide bombs. The author sensed during subsequent visits to the PAF, that it was a concern for the leadership. Undeterred, they set about training to fight the Rafale and the European BVRAAM. In 2020, the PAF ordered both the long-range PL-15 and short-range PL-10 missiles which could be a game changer against the Meteor.

The PAF's new tactics development school went into overdrive, employing the PAC/Chengdu JF-17 and Lockheed Martin F-16s against Rafales in simulations. Every possible avenue was exploited to understand the weaknesses of the French jet.

Asked if the air forces of Qatar or Egypt had helped with this? ACM Sidhu said: "No. Because neither side fly the Rafale in the same tactical manner as India does."

In the 1990s, before the PAF took delivery of the AIM-120 AMRAAM, it concentrated on within visual range (WVR) tactics, and according to the RAF and USAF pilots the author had talked to after exercises with them, they were very good at it. But it was different now.

Multi domain warfare

When ACM Sidhu became PAF Chief of the Air Staff on March 19, 2021, he ushered in some very big changes, realising the importance of different challenges of Air Power, and wanted to confront them through indigenous efforts.

On the operational side, he invested time and resources into new domains like cyber, electronic warfare and space, as well as ground-based air defences and unmanned aerial vehicles. He would then integrate them with the operational fighters in what he refers to as 'multi domain warfare'.

In June 2021, just three months after taking office, ACM Sidhu ordered 20, now much-prized Chengdu J-10Cs from China. They would be armed with the very long-range PL-15 and shorter-range PL-10 air-to-air missiles. The first

This Operation Swift Retort memorial at Mushaf, heralds the work of the based aggressors which claimed the shoot down of a Su-30MKI Flanker and highly publicised MiG-21 Bison

A J-10C sits on the edge of the 15 (Multi Role) Squadron shelter area, armed and looking very dangerous, Clearly visible is the IRST sensor on the nose and the air-to-air refuelling probe PAF

launched a sweeping offensive, crippling 96% of India's social networks, penetrating critical systems, and even disrupting the country's railways, airlines, banks and energy grids to sow chaos. Bold messages flashed across Indian CCTV screens, while websites were defaced and key digital nodes were struck, triggering electricity blackouts across vast regions of India. This was the first time any Air Force in the world had synced its cyber operations with its kinetic operations.

PAF Cyber Ops had shifted into offensive mode. Back in 2019 during Operation Swift Retort, there was no cyber footprint, but by 2021 work had commenced on creating the new command, which opened in May 2023 and started functioning in October 2024. PAF has created a cyber range, where cyber warfare skills are built up by pitching blue and red teams against each other. Elements of the PAF Cyber Force played an active role in achieving the right effects during Op Bunyan-un-Marsoos, when cyber was integrated with kinetic ops. PAF kept it all relevant by participating in operations and exercises like Indus Shield 24.

Breaking the news

News on this clash broke in Europe later that day (May 7) when the ISPR held a press conference.

The PAF's Deputy Chief of Air Staff (DCAS Operations) and Director General Public Relations (DGPR) took much of the world by surprise, when they claimed the PAF had shot down five IAF fighters. These included three, later increased to four, extremely capable 4.5-generation Rafales fitted with the cutting-edge Thales Spectra electronic warfare systems. The air-to-air kills were backed up by images from social media accounts and included GPS co-ordinates of where they crashed.

As the PAF's DCAS Ops disclosed at the press conference, attended by both local and international media, the IAF were continuously

scrambling their fighters in the early hours, to reinforce and saturate the air defence. "Our strategy was to have force concentration in our selected AORs and fight to our own strength.

"Once they saw our numbers, the IAF fighters launched their ground weapons, and we identified them. As soon as this happened, the Chief changed the rules of engagement from 'deter' to 'sure kill'.

"We targeted the Rafales, because the IAF had always said they would make 'the difference'."

The DCAS (Ops) talked with the aid of a screen at the conference about the losses and the locations where they were shot down. The PAF had tapped into IAF Rafale communications, and listened to a four-ship 'Godzilla 1-4' formation in panic and distress, having discovered one of the French jets was missing.

He ran the recordings to assembled media, which was quite startling at the time, but it seems the Rafale pilots were mistakenly talking on an open frequency rather than a secure one. During the stand-off, the PAF identified 14 Rafales within the 72 aircraft, through its electronic intelligence systems, and then targeted them.

The PAF also struck the radar in the northern ICCS (Integrated Command and Control Centre) at Barnala which effectively stopped all communications between the IAF leadership and their fighters.

The Indian military fired Brahmos air/surface-to-ground missiles capable of speeds of 3,000km/h (1,900mph) one after the other. I was told by the PAF there had been 'soft kills' and 'hard kills' by the Brahmos. There is some suggestion the PAF jammed the Brahmos frequencies but no one would confirm this.

During the press briefing, the PAF spokesperson showed the radar signatures of the Brahmos on the screen, which he said missed targets and flew into Afghanistan.

After 52 minutes, the IAF fighters fled back to their bases, outwitted by the PAF. A senior officer, told the author: "The Rafale is potent

Wg Cdr Bilal, Flight Cdr, Ops 15 Squadron, banks his jet to show off the four PL-15 missiles on the twin racks and single PL-10 on the outside hard points. The potent PL-15 struck a Rafale nearly 200km away. Alan Warnes

Armed and very dangerous

'Cobras redefined' – the 15 Squadron patch worn by the J-10C pilots

A highly acclaimed J-10C Vigorous Dragon patch

Another PAF J-10C patch signifying two roles

The JF-17C Block 3s were armed with the PL-10 and PL-15s, which was not publicly acknowledged until just before India attacked Pakistan. They never shot down an Indian Air Force jet during Pakistan's Operation Bunyan-un-Marsoos, probably because the jet's KLJ-7A radar does not match the range of the J-10C's KLJ-10 PAF

enough, and while we initially declared we had shot down three, BS001 [17 Sqn], BS022, BS027 [both 101 Sqn], we also had it confirmed by HUMINT [human intelligence] in mid-July that BS021 [from 101 Sqn] had been confirmed as shot down, over Srinagar."

The author understands another four aircraft have not returned to the flightline. The PAF has their tail numbers, because they know from their electronic intelligence the jets that were badly damaged. They are endeavouring to confirm from OSINT (Open-Source Intelligence/HUMINT – often spies on the ground). The PAF refrained from attacking further than 2,000km (1,250 miles) away because it felt it could start an all-out war.

Rafale kills

The author, understandably, wanted to know how the PAF could identify the downed aircraft, as many of the Indian public will not believe it. As a retired officer explained: "In

A close-up of an Indian Air Force Rafale kill on the side of a J-10C in mid-July PAF

No 29 Squadron is the PAF's Aggressor squadron, that commenced flying operations on January 23, 2019, just before Op Swift Retort took place on February 27, 2019. It is an integral part of the ACE facility, playing Red Air during exercises like Saffron Bandit and Indus Viper. The J-10C pilots have also trained as Aggressors and will undoubtedly be a big attraction for foreign air forces attending Indus Viper next year

this BVR war, it's very difficult to show the wreckage of the jet you have shot down, because they fell in Indian territory. Although there were many images appearing on social media, our foe will never admit it, so what we do is judge the 'kill' with different parameters as most air forces do.

"Our Identification (ID) Matrix is a structured process that ensures accuracy, accountability, and verification in air combat operations. It begins with the detection of an aircraft radar, followed by its positive identification within the Comprehensive Complete Air Picture (CCAP) at the command centre, where every Indian aircraft is clearly tagged and tracked.

"Once detection is confirmed, the next step involves assessing the lock parameters of the missile system, which can only engage a target within specific speed, range and angular limits. After securing a lock on the target, the missile is launched, and its progress is monitored through radar tracking. If the target's radar signature disappears from the CCAP screen, it is registered as a 'probable kill'.

"However, the process does not end there, upon returning to base, the pilot undergoes a thorough debrief in which the mission video recording is reviewed to validate that the missile engagement met all required parameters – direction, speed, lock range and envelope. This Multilayered ID Matrix not only guarantees the precision of engagements but also ensures transparency and post-mission verification, making it a cornerstone of the PAF's credibility in confirming air-to-air victories. Once these steps had been processed, the PAF tried to confirm the 'kills' by OSINT/HUMINT."

None of the above could be done without the seamless integration of radar inputs from multiple field radars and sector headquarters to create the CCAP at Command HQ. This process by the PAF ensures that data from geographically dispersed radars is fused into one unified, real-time operational display. Instead of each radar working in isolation, their coverage areas are digitally overlapped and synchronised, eliminating gaps and blind spots. The PAF achieves 360° surveillance of national airspace, enabling commanders to track, identify, and prioritise aerial threats with precision. It enhances situational awareness by filtering and corelating radar feeds, thereby reducing the duplication or misinterpretation of targets. As the senior officer told the author: "[Radar] Knitting symbolises the transition from localised radar control to network-centric defence system, empowering the PAF to maintain air superiority through unified awareness, co-ordinated response, and robust command and control."

The PAF provided the Rafale tail numbers, BS001, BS021, BS022 and BS027 to allow Dassault an opportunity to clarify if the aircraft was still current. Much of the Indian population and news channels still refuse to believe the Rafales were shot down, but while the IAF refutes these allegations, they have yet to provide post-May 7 images of the four jets with the serial numbers and close ups of their manufacturers' serial number.

Dassault has remained tight-lipped, although it did quite unusually put out a press release denying that its CEO Eric Trappier had said "no Rafales were shot down" after this was circulating on social media.

Sources told the author: "We have video recordings of the downed aircraft and battle damage assessment imagery which we intend to release at the time of our own choosing and when we deem it appropriate which will cause further embarrassment to the IAF."

Indian acknowledgement

The Indian Chief of Defence Staff, General Anil Chauhan, admitted to Bloomberg Television on May 31, that IAF jets had been shot down that night. He denied Pakistan's tally of six but declined to specify the exact number. "What is important is not the jet being [shot] down, but why they were downed," Chauhan said. "Numbers are not important."

He admitted tactical mistakes were made during the conflict, although he observed that

the Indian military did carry out long-range precision strikes on targeted installations.

Chauhan finished: "The good part is that we are able to understand the tactical mistakes, remedy them, and implement them again."

His admission was overshadowed by a bolder statement from a political heavyweight in India, Subramanian Swamy, who acknowledged the loss of at least five Indian aircraft during the clash.

On August 9, Indian Air Force commander Marshal Amar Preet Singh, who has been in office since September 2024, prompted

The Saab 2000 Erieye was the unsung hero of Op Bunyan-un-Marsoos, supporting the situational requirements of the fighter packages

ripples of disbelief while addressing an Air Force Association gathering in Bangalore by saying: "We shot down five PAF fighters and an AEW&C Erieye with our S-400 SAMs at a range of 300 kilometres."

Coming three months after the battle had concluded, it not only contradicted the earlier admission by his superior, General Chauhan, but also lacked any supporting evidence.

It appeared to be a desperate attempt to placate Prime Minister Modi, whose government has been under mounting pressure to mask the scale of the IAF's losses. The stark contradiction between India's top military leaders underscores the turbulence within its defence establishment.

Training to fight Rafale

The IAF had bought 36 Dassault Rafales in 2016, along with MBDA Meteor BVRAAMs, MBDA Scalp EG/Storm Shadow cruise missiles and Safran AASM Hammer glide bombs. The author sensed during subsequent visits to the PAF, that it was a concern for the leadership. Undeterred, they set about training to fight the Rafale and the European BVRAAM. In 2020, the PAF ordered both the long-range PL-15 and short-range PL-10 missiles which could be a game changer against the Meteor.

The PAF's new tactics development school went into overdrive, employing the PAC/Chengdu JF-17 and Lockheed Martin F-16s against Rafales in simulations. Every possible avenue was exploited to understand the weaknesses of the French jet.

Asked if the air forces of Qatar or Egypt had helped with this? ACM Sidhu said: "No. Because neither side fly the Rafale in the same tactical manner as India does."

In the 1990s, before the PAF took delivery of the AIM-120 AMRAAM, it concentrated on within visual range (WVR) tactics, and according to the RAF and USAF pilots the author had talked to after exercises with them, they were very good at it. But it was different now.

Multi domain warfare

When ACM Sidhu became PAF Chief of the Air Staff on March 19, 2021, he ushered in some very big changes, realising the importance of different challenges of Air Power, and wanted to confront them through indigenous efforts.

On the operational side, he invested time and resources into new domains like cyber, electronic warfare and space, as well as ground-based air defences and unmanned aerial vehicles. He would then integrate them with the operational fighters in what he refers to as 'multi domain warfare'.

In June 2021, just three months after taking office, ACM Sidhu ordered 20, now much-prized Chengdu J-10Cs from China. They would be armed with the very long-range PL-15 and shorter-range PL-10 air-to-air missiles. The first

This Operation Swift Retort memorial at Mushaf, heralds the work of the based aggressors which claimed the shoot down of a Su-30MKI Flanker and highly publicised MiG-21 Bison

six J-10Cs arrived on March 4, 2022. A multi-domain operations centre (MDOC) and a National ISR Air Ops Centre (NIIAOC) were two of many new departments the Commander created, where along with his staff and personnel, he could watch all these new assets interlinked while controlling the PAF's every move.

At the same time, the Airpower Combat Employment (ACE) facility at PAF Base Mushaf, created in 2016, was upgraded considerably into one of the best tactical training ranges in the world. In 2023 it was relabelled the Aerospace Power Centre of Excellence (ACE).

ACE is where PAF pilots and GCIs can test their capabilities and skills against each other and with international allies during Indus Shield exercises. Two have taken place to date, in 2023 and 2024. During the latter, 24 nations, including observers, participated with Royal Saudi Air Force Tornados, Turkish Air Force F-16C/Ds and Egypt F-16Cs present.

A senior officer told me: "We embraced fifth-dimensional warfare, with a highly effective cyber force that we built with support from the National Aerospace Science Technology Park [NASTP]. The aim is to support PAF ops, both kinetic and non-kinetic effects. We practice everything at ACE."

NASTP is an interesting development, a bold leap into the future that wasn't even an idea when the author last visited in 2020, where academia, industry and the government are linked together through an impressive ecosystem. It isn't just a technology park for innovation; it has been created to pursue the Air Chief's vision of a launchpad for strategic autonomy.

The level of intelligence being gleaned from India through different domains, as the author observed at the NIIAOC, is quite unbelievable. The author was allowed exclusive access to the facility, where even the most senior officers are often not allowed to visit.

Every Indian base could be monitored, every aircraft from the moment of lift-off in Western Command was tracked. There are Pakistani eyes everywhere. During my time with the PAF it was obvious there was nothing the PAF didn't know about the IAF.

From the start of the contingency op and as the tension with India escalated, the PAF Commander made the command centre his home, snatching sleep whenever possible on a mattress in a side room. He said he felt it was a once-in-a-lifetime opportunity and he didn't want to miss anything.

Alongside him in the command centre were the heads of all the new integrated domains, EW, Cyber and Space; there were air defence controllers, along with the head of the main kinetic force – the fighters in the air. He consulted with them, before making decisions in what the PAF calls 'centralised control and decentralised execution'.

Several officers who worked with the CAS, told the author how the 'boss', as they refer to him, took the lead on everything, even telling the J-10C pilots when and where to fire.

Indian strikes then a response

According to the IAF, retaliatory strikes took place at 11 different military air bases, on May 10. The bases included PAF Base Nur Khan near Rawalpindi, which was, according to the PAF, struck by Spice 2000 PGMs released by Mirage 2000s. It missed the HQ-9 missile battery at the facility.

Rafiqui was also struck, as was a hangar at PAF Base Murid, the home to four squadrons of UAVs, and the runway at Rahim Yar airfield that the IAF says plays a strategic role in Pakistan's air defences, but is a civil airport used by the UAE Royal family for hunting trips.

PAF Base Bholari was subjected to an attack on one of its hangars, that claimed the lives of five PAF personnel and damaged a Saab 2000 Erieye that the PAF says has been repaired. The runway at PAF Base Mushaf was struck but was made operational again within a few hours.

A close-up of the 29 Squadron memorial, giving all the names of the pilots on the unit during Op Swift Retort. The OC, Wg Cdr Nouman Ali Khan, shot down the IAF MiG-21 Bison with an AIM-120 AMRAAM 'Slammer' while flying a 11 Squadron jet

The 29 Squadron Aggressors' patch

A 16 Squadron JF-17C Thunder Block 3 taxies back to the unit's shelter area at Kamra-Minhas. The Black Panthers played a major part in the air defence of Pakistan on May 6/7 *PAF*

"They were sitting ducks - they didn't stand a chance when our J-10Cs unleashed those PL-15s."

In retaliation to the IAF offensive and loss of civilian lives, the PAF sent indigenous killer drones assembled by the NASTP into India flying over the bases at Adampur, Agra, Bhantral, Bhatwala, Bhuj, Gujrat, Srinagar and even the capital, Delhi, where they flew orbits overhead, packed with 20kg explosives. The drones with PAF's homegrown front and back-end technologies were not met with any resistance because the IAF's air defences had been blocked, and as a result the IAF was practically grounded.

Over the next few hours on May 10 the PAF hit 34 targets on different bases, half were by fighters, the rest were struck by the killer drones. While the PAF was initially aggressive, everything became measured, and more could have been taken out, according to a PAF senior officer, who told me they even had a lock on a A-50 AWACS lining up at Agra, but the attack was stopped, according to the PAF, so the IAF could save face.

For seven days, after the strikes ended, only one aircraft flew from Western Command and that was a Rafale that dropped a Scalp EG/Storm Shadow cruise missile, working with an A-50 AWACS.

SEAD

One of the biggest threats to the PAF, alongside the Rafale, is the mobile S-400 air defence system. They needed them to be destroyed, because they are extremely dangerous. So much so, the PAF was monitoring their every move in Western Command – at Adampur, Bhuj and Bikaner.

The S-400 is a long-range Russian mobile surface-to-air missile (SAM) system - the SA-21 *Growler* - designed to destroy a wide range of aerial threats, including ballistic missiles, cruise missiles, aircraft and drones. It is considered one of the most advanced SAMs in the world, capable of engaging multiple targets simultaneously. Most NATO fighter forces train to counter the S-400 and will be very interested in how the PAF fared. The system has a range of up to 400km (250 miles), engage targets up to 100,000ft (30km) and track up to 300 targets, engaging 36 of them simultaneously. It is deadly.

The PAF was not keen to share the S-400's MAR (the distance from which the SAM can hit its target). Needless to say, the JF-17s needed to get close to the range of the S-400 to fire its two long-range supersonic Chinese-made CM-400AKG missiles.

In the early morning of May 10, a JF-17C Thunder Block 3 of 14 Sqn 'Tail Choppers' departed Rafiqui on a deadly Destruction of Enemy Air Defence (DEAD) mission, to destroy the S-400 system deployed to Adampur. As the JF-17 headed towards the target, the S-400's radars were being saturated by a substantial amount of jamming and other electronic warfare methods. At the same time, the JF-17 was spitting out decoys coupled with evasive manoeuvres.

As it got inside the S-400's firing range, the pilot was ordered to fire his CM400AKGs. He flew well inside the Rafale's Meteor's MAR but thankfully for the pilot, there was no resistance.

According to the PAF, the CM-400AKGs scored a direct hit on the 'Cheese Board' low altitude tracker and 'Big Bird' early warning and broad surveillance radars, and as a result put the S-400 missile launchers out of action. Three days later, the Indian PM, Narendra Modi, visited Adampur AFS, where he posed for a photo in front of a S-400 missile system to show that it was still operational. But as the PAF Commander said: "They didn't show him with the radar systems – without them it is useless."

The CM-400AKG is China's long-range air-launched air-to-ground weapon, powered by a solid-fuel rocket that can reach supersonic speeds of Mach 5. It is passive, so doesn't need to be guided onto the target by radar. The range of the S-400 missiles (up to 400km) is the same as the JF-17's CM-400AKG.

As the senior officer told me: "To get inside the range of an S-400 radar and come back alive is quite an achievement because you are giving the missile a chance to shoot you down. You must employ your game plan and the maximum range you can go. We employ scenarios through ACE and Combat Commanders School (CCS), flying them regularly again and again as we do on the squadrons." So, what happened was no different than what the PAF had trained for. Similarly, the PAF gave a crippling blow to the IAF by destroying the IACCS at Barnala.

Cobras

No 15 'Cobras' Squadron and its J-10Cs played a massive part in defeating India's ambitions on May 7. It is testimony to the way they train, that the pilots who went into battle only had between 100 and 120 hours on the Chinese jet. During the three years in service, they had spent much of their time devoted to air-to-air combat training in the likes of 2v2, 4v4, 8x8, 10v8 scenarios.

The current office commanding (OC), who for security reasons did not want to be identified, said: "In a relatively short span of three to four years, the PAF has inducted a new generation aircraft. While the Chinese have operated the J-10 for two decades, they haven't employed it the way we have and that's because of the PAF's training. The best pilots were recruited from the F-16 Viper and JF-17 Thunder forces and transferred to the J-10.

The IAF received their Rafales years before the PAF received its J-10s (the first five were delivered in July 2020) and they had more (36) too.

Incredibly, the six pilots who went to Chengdu in China to train on the J-10C, flew just two to three hours before ferrying six jets back to Kamra-Minhas in March 2022.

The PAF needed them quickly because of the rising Rafale threat, and within nine months they were operational. Much of that time was spent mastering the tactical sensors, working in all the different spectrums, including air-to-air refuelling. It took the PAF just eight months to get the jets to Pakistan after the contract was signed. Compare that to the Rafale in India, and the five to six years it took from contract signature to being operational.

The J-10C's KLJ-10 Active Electronically Scanned Array (AESA) radar improves detection and targeting in environments that pose a longer range over the F-16C Block 52's older mechanically scanned AN/APG-68 radar system, allowing the J-10C to engage targets from a much greater distance. PAF J-10Cs reached fully operational capability by early 2023 and were involved in a national level exercise the same year. The threats that PAF can simulate in J-10Cs are unlike anywhere else in the world.

The PAF's 'Radar Knitting' and 'ID Matrix' processes were extremely good during the air battle, while the rules of engagement were very clear, something that the IAF lacked in the conflict.

The 15 Sqn OC continued: "The CAS has brought ACE on a lot since 2016, back then it was more Air Power, than Aerospace and was more rudimentary for the pilots and fighter controllers. Now it includes air battle management and GBADs [ground-based air defences] and there is an operational interface with the Joint Strike Simulation Centre at ACE."

The author visited the ACE's Joint Services command and Staff College (JSSC) where students develop game plans, with air defence assets like GBADs alongside radars, electro-optical sensors and passive sensors enabling recognised air pictures. They then run it, to see how it works before they flew the mission. In the first international Indus Shield exercise at ACE in 2023, 14 countries attended and on the second in 2024 there were 24. A former Turkish Air Force F-35 pilot, now an F-16 Sqn Commander, told the OC 15 Sqn: "Indus Shield is similar to the USAF's Red Flag and in some domains better. vThe PAF is now working in a multi domain warfare and while very aggressive, they are disciplined."

Pakistan and India have already fought each other in two wars, since Pakistan gained independence in 1947. There have also been two major skirmishes between the PAF and IAF – Kargil in 1999 and Swift Retort in 2019, but this latest confrontation, that saw the biggest BVR air war ever witnessed anywhere in the world, is a sign that nothing will change anytime soon. With tension running high between the two nations, things could even get worse… **afm**

About the author

I have visited the Pakistan Air Force over 20 times, since first going to Pakistan in May 2001. I had not visited since 2020, due to family reasons and because the PAF was going through huge modernisation. This year, facilitated by the support of veterans and senior officers, I re-established my association with the PAF and had the privilege of visiting various facilities in July.

From being primarily fighter-centric when I last visited, the PAF has now emerged as a full-spectrum, multi-domain force operating seamlessly across space, cyber, artificial intelligence, drone warfare and integrated kinetic air power. As a result, the PAF I have observed now stands as a contemporary, forward-looking air force that is ready to meet the challenges of modern warfare head-on.

The author, Alan Warnes

Two JF-17C Thunder Block 3 of 8 Squadron 'Haiders' attended the Royal International Air Tattoo in July, and surrounded the specially marked jet with all the weapons in its inventory. This included the PL-15 and PL-10, as well as the large CM-400AKG seen here on the right Ben Stanley Hall

Calling
for Carriers!

As HMS *Prince of Wales* (R09) and the wider UK Carrier Strike Group prepares to embark on its highly anticipated CSG-25 deployment to the Indo-Pacific later this year, **Khalem Chapman** looks back on the UK's naval renaissance and provides an operational overview on the Royal Navy's latest 'flattops'

As the largest and most powerful warships to have ever entered fleet service with the Royal Navy, the UK's two new, Queen Elizabeth-class aircraft carriers – HMS *Queen Elizabeth* (R08) and her sister warship, HMS *Prince of Wales* (R09) – formed the alluring centrepiece of Britain's much-needed naval renaissance when they were formally commissioned in 2017 and 2019, respectively.

Their arrival beckoned the rebirth of the Navy's Carrier Strike capabilities, bringing with them a host of new, cutting-edge aircraft to form one of the most advanced carrier air wings (CVW) in the world.

From December 2010, Britain rapidly lost its ability to effectively project carrier-based combat airpower as a result of the highly controversial 2010 Strategic Defence and Security Review (SDSR). The UK's Carrier Strike community suffered significant losses, with the Joint Force Harrier fleet being axed on December 15, 2010. The first of the Navy's two remaining Invincible-class aircraft carriers, HMS *Ark Royal* (R07), was decommissioned on March 11, 2011, followed by HMS *Invincible* (R06), having been retained as a helicopter carrier, on August 28, 2014.

As the UK's older Carrier Strike assets were pushed into an early retirement, construction

of the first Queen Elizabeth-class 'flattop' was starting to progress at the Rosyth Dockyard in Fife, Scotland. With the first steel being cut for the project on July 7, 2009, the warship was christened HMS *Queen Elizabeth* (*QE*) on July 4, 2014, before being formally launched on July 17. After a period of sea trials, *QE* was commissioned into service at HM Naval Base Portsmouth, Hampshire, on December 7, 2017, plugging the three-year capability gap caused by the withdrawal of *Invincible* in 2014.

Construction of the second Queen Elizabeth-class carrier got under way on May 26, 2011. The warship was formally christened HMS *Prince of Wales* (*POW*) on September 8, 2017, before being launched on December 21, that year. Following initial sea trials, *POW* was commissioned into fleet service at Portsmouth on December 10, 2019.

As the first-in-class 'flattop', *QE* conducted the majority of rotary and fixed-wing flight trials for the UK's new-generation carrier force. In a phased manner, initial helicopter trials began in early 2018, followed by fixed-wing flight testing with the F-35B off the US East Coast as part of the WESTLANT 18 and 19 deployments in late 2018 and late 2019, respectively.

On completion, the UK's renewed and highly modernised Carrier Strike capabilities were tested during *QE's* first operational deployment to the Indo-Pacific as part of Operation Fortis (or Carrier Strike Group-21, CSG-21) from May-December 2021. Having entered operational fleet service some two years after *QE*, *POW* had spent the best part of her career so far preparing for her own maiden deployment, which is scheduled to begin in April leading the UK's CSG-25 to the Indo-Pacific.

A new age

Measuring 284m (923ft) long and 73m (240ft) wide with an empty displacement of 65,000 tonnes – rising to an estimated 80,600 tonnes at full load – the new 'flattops' are the largest warships ever to lead the British fleet. Both are roughly three times the size of the previous Invincible-class carriers, which displaced 22,000 tonnes (empty).

Operationally speaking, the flight decks of both 'flattops' are far more accommodating, being 280m (919ft) long, 70m (230ft) wide and nearly twice the size of the decks carried by their predecessors. While the Invincible-class 'flattops' had a capacity for up to 22 aircraft, their successors can be surged to carry a maximum of 72, if required. Until December 2010, the UK embarked a Carrier Air Group that – depending on mission requirements – typically comprised between 12-18 Harrier GR7/GR9 fighters and four to ten Sea King ASaC7 airborne early warning (AEW) helicopters or Merlin HM1 anti-submarine/surface warfare (ASW/ASuW) rotorcraft – platforms that would now be deemed relatively obsolete by the capability standards of modern warfare.

Britain's maritime renaissance not only provided two cutting-edge 'flattops', but also a new, highly modernised CVW. Together, these fifth-generation naval assets will project UK military power/influence on the global stage for the next half-century, be it to deter potential aggressors, respond to crises or to support Westminster's diplomatic/political objectives and interests. The CVW aboard these carriers also comprises some of the most advanced aircraft to have been developed for carrier-borne operations to date.

While both warships can be surged to carry up to 72 aircraft during wartime, a routine

*Left: **An historic moment in the UK's decade-long carrier renaissance occurred on May 19, 2021, when HMS Queen Elizabeth (R08) – seen carrying a mix of F-35Bs from the RAF-badged No 617 Squadron 'The Dambusters' and USMC's VMFA-211 'Wake Island Avengers' (above) – sailed alongside her sister warship, HMS Prince of Wales (R09), for the first time** MOD Crown Copyright/ POPhot Jay Allen*

*Below: **The UK welcomed the return of its dormant Carrier Strike capabilities on June 20, 2021, when two UKLF F-35Bs (ZM147/'013' and ZM154/'020') carried out the type's first operational mission over the Middle East in support of Operation Shader, while operating from QE during the CSG-21 cruise. British F-35Bs currently carry Paveway IV LGBs, AMRAAMs and ASRAAMs, but this arsenal will soon be expanded to include the Meteor BVRAAM and SPEAR 3 miniature cruise missile** MOD Crown Copyright/Cpl Lee Matthews*

An RAF-operated Chinook HC5 (ZH902) is trialled on the aircraft lift aboard QE in February 2018. The carrier's two aircraft lifts can raise two F-35Bs or a single Chinook (without folded blades) from the hangar to the flight deck in approximately 60 seconds MOD Crown Copyright

> ## "The new CSG is the embodiment of British maritime power and sits at the heart of a modernised and emboldened Royal Navy"
> Cdre Steve Moorhouse, Commander of the UK CSG (2018-2022)

peacetime cruise would typically see no more than 40 embark aboard. Both can carry a total of 36 short take-off and vertical landing (STOVL)-capable F-35B Lightnings, but only 12-24 examples of the fifth-generation multi-role fighter would deploy during peacetime (see 'Lightnings on deck').

Alongside the F-35Bs, the 'flattops' can also embark several different rotorcraft, including two distinct versions of the Merlin HM2 – with the baseline version tasked with the ASW mission and Crowsnest Airborne Surveillance and Control (ASaC) role kit-fitted examples covering the AEW role (see 'Multi-mission Merlins'). Both ships can also accommodate the 'Commando' Merlin HC4s, when required.

Each carrier is also capable of embarking both variants of the nimble Wildcat multi-mission battlefield utility helicopters, comprising the 'Commando' Wildcat AH1s and the ASW/ASuW-configured Wildcat HMA2s (see 'On the prowl'). They can also carry RAF-operated Chinook HC5 tactical transport helicopters and the Army Air Corps' (AAC) new Apache AH2 gunships, which are used to support UK Commando Helicopter Force (CHF) operations (see 'Going Commando').

Assembling the fleet

On June 26, 2017, *QE* departed Rosyth for initial sea trials. While not yet capable of conducting sustained flight operations, it did not take long for the first helicopter – a Merlin HM2 from the Fleet Air Arm's (FAA) 820 Naval Air Squadron (NAS) – to grace her newly forged flight deck on July 3.

After completing a successful period of phased flight trials from 2018 to 2020, the *QE* was advancing towards Initial Operational Capability (IOC). On September 21, 2020, it departed Portsmouth to participate in the UK-led multinational training drill, Exercise Joint Warrior 20-2 (JW 20-2), which was crucial for *QE's* upcoming IOC declaration and preparing the UK CSG for its first global deployment.

Lightnings on deck

Operated as a pooled fighting force from RAF Marham, Norfolk, the UK Lightning Force (UKLF) currently fields 31 F-35Bs across three squadrons, staffed by a mix of RAF and Fleet Air Arm (FAA) personnel. The force comprises two operational frontline units – the RAF's No 617 Squadron 'The Dambusters' and the FAA's 809 Naval Air Squadron (NAS) 'Immortals' – while the Air Force-badged No 207 Squadron serves as the Operational Conversion Unit (OCU).

As is the case with both *QE* and *POW*, the F-35B is very much in the early stages of its evolution. Currently, it can deliver a hard-hitting punch using Paveway IV LGBs against surface targets and AMRAAM/ASRAAMs against airborne threats. Facilitated by the Technology Refresh 3 (TR-3) update, the type's highly anticipated Block 4 upgrade – set to begin later this decade – will add the Meteor BVRAAM and SPEAR 3 miniature cruise missile to its growing arsenal, making it even more lethal.

While the UK remains "committed" to acquiring 138 F-35Bs in total, just 48 jets have been ordered to date. The UK has received 35 of the 48 F-35Bs ordered in its initial Tranche 1 procurement phase, although one aircraft was lost during the Fortis deployment in 2021. Another three jets were retained by No 17 Test and Evaluation Squadron (TES) at Edwards AFB, California, for ongoing test activities, but these jets will soon be sent to Marham to join the wider operational fleet.

The UKLF expects to receive its final Tranche 1 F-35Bs before declaring full operational capability (FOC) before the end of this year. A second batch of 27 aircraft is expected to be ordered in the Tranche 2 procurement phase, with the aim of growing the fleet to 74 F-35Bs by the end of this decade.

Above: Personnel from QE's Air Engineering Department prepare a Paveway IV LGB for an F-35B live-fire exercise on October 5, 2023. Both carriers are fitted with a Highly Mechanised Weapon Handling System (HMWHS), which uses a network of tracks and remote-controlled 'moles' to move pallets of munitions to weapon preparation areas, the hangar or flight deck via a series of hydraulic lifts that run through the heart of the warship MOD Crown Copyright/LPhot Belinda Alker

Leading from the front! QE leads the rest of CSG-21 back to the UK during the final stages of Operation Fortis on October 19, 2021 MOD Crown Copyright/LPhot Unaisi Luke

QE embarked her largest number of aircraft for JW 20-2, including eight Merlin HM2/HC4s from the FAA's 820/845 NAS and 14 F-35Bs from the UK Lightning Force (UKLF) – namely the world-famous 'Dambusters' of No 617 Squadron and the USMC's Marine Fighter Attack Squadron 211 (VMFA-211) 'Wake Island Avengers'. This marked the largest group of fifth-generation jets to be deployed at-sea and the biggest concentration of fighters to embark aboard a British carrier since the Centaur-class light carrier, HMS *Hermes* (R12), completed her last operational cruise in 1983.

JW 20-2 was the first time a full CSG was formed around the UK's new carriers, offering an early glimpse of the strike group's force posture before the Operation Fortis deployment in 2021. It also provided *QE* and her CVW with an opportunity to conduct training and integration activities alongside her escort vessels ahead of the carrier's first operational cruise.

The exercise involved several other British warships, including the Type 45 (Daring-class) air-defence destroyers, HMS *Diamond* (D34) and HMS *Defender* (D36); Type 23 (Duke-class) frigates, HMS *Kent* (F78) and HMS *Northumberland* (F238); and an unnamed nuclear submarine. The Royal Fleet Auxiliary (RFA) supplied two replenishment oilers with the presence of the Tide-class RFA *Tideforce* (A139) and Fort-class RFA *Fort Victoria* (A387). The UK CSG was also joined by the US Navy's Arleigh Burke-class guided-missile destroyer, USS *The Sullivans* (DDG-68), and the Royal Netherlands Navy's De Zeven Provinciën-class frigate, HNLMS *Evertsen* (F805).

All of these ships – except *Northumberland* and *Tideforce*, which were replaced by HMS *Richmond* (F239) and RFA *Tidespring* (A136), respectively – later joined the *QE*-led CSG-21 during Operation Fortis, along with the nuclear-powered Astute-class attack submarine, HMS *Astute* (S119).

As this new-look strike group first assembled during JW 20-2 in September 2020, Cdre Steve Moorhouse, Commander of the UK CSG, declared: "The UK's maritime renaissance has been unfolding over many years, as we introduced a new generation of ships, submarines and aircraft into service. But this marks the first time we have brought them together in a cohesive, potent fighting force. The new CSG is the embodiment of British maritime power and sits at the heart of a modernised and emboldened Royal Navy.

"Protected by a ring of advanced destroyers, frigates, helicopters and submarines, and equipped with fifth-generation fighters, [*QE*] is able to strike from the sea at a time and place of our choosing, and with our NATO allies at our side, we will be ready to fight and win in the most demanding circumstances… Carrier Strike offers Britain choice and flexibility on the global stage; it reassures our friends and allies and presents a powerful deterrent to would-be adversaries."

After completing JW 20-2, *QE* returned to Portsmouth on October 15, 2020. The Navy formally declared IOC on its new flagship on January 4, 2021. She then conducted final work-up and aircrew carrier qualification activities before leading CSG-21 to the Far East during Fortis.

Five Merlin HC4s from 845 NAS 'Junglies' and a single Wildcat AH1 from 847 NAS fly back to Yeovilton after parting ways with the UK CSG following the conclusion of the seven-month Operation Fortis (CSG-21) cruise on December 8, 2021. These aircraft are a vital part of the CHF and while they can embark aboard the carriers, they will typically operate from escort vessels during CSG deployments MOD Crown Copyright

Above: **This F-35B (ZM154/'020') demonstrates the fifth-generation multi-role stealth fighter's unique STOVL configuration while preparing to land aboard POW after completing a mission as part of Exercise Nordic Response 24 on March 5, 2024** *MOD Crown Copyright/AS1 Amber Mayall*

Below: **The Navy has procured ten Crowsnest ASaC role kits for its Merlin HM2 fleet. At least five helicopters will be configured for AEW operations at any given time, with three 'frontline' aircraft being assigned to the high-readiness carrier and the remaining two being used for training/evaluation work at Culdrose** *MOD Crown Copyright/AS1 Amber Mayall*

Three WAH-64D Apache AH1 gunships from No 656 Squadron – a part of the AAC's 4 Regiment at Wattisham Flying Station, Suffolk – land aboard POW to conduct integration training with the new Queen Elizabeth-class aircraft carrier in June 2021. The latest version of the gunship, the AH-64E(V6) Apache AH2, has yet to embark on the 'flattops' *MOD Crown Copyright*

Leading from the front

In April 2021, the CVW gathered for its first long-term operational deployment aboard *QE*. Ten F-35Bs from the USMC's VMFA-211 arrived at RAF Lakenheath, Suffolk, from April 26-28. They remained there until May 2 and the following day, eight UKLF F-35Bs – with crews drawn from 'The Dambusters' – joined their US counterparts on the carrier.

Meanwhile, 820 NAS deployed seven Merlin HM2s aboard *QE* on April 27, comprising four ASW-configured helicopters and three Crowsnest ASaC aircraft. On May 1, four Wildcat HMA2s from 815 NAS embarked on each of *QE*'s escort vessels (*Diamond*, *Defender*, *Kent* and *Richmond*), while three Merlin HC4s from 845 NAS arrived aboard *Fort Victoria* on May 3.

Before departing for the Far East, CSG-21 participated in Exercise Strike Warrior 21-1 (SW 21-1) – the maritime element of the UK-led Exercise Joint Warrior 21-1 – off the Scottish coast from May 8-19. The training drill involved around 13,400 personnel, 150 aircraft, 31 warships and three submarines from ten different NATO nations. It marked the first deployment of the Crowsnest-equipped Merlins and UKLF F-35Bs – equipped with Advanced Short-Range Air-to-Air Missiles (ASRAAMs) – conducting the first fast-jet live-fire operations from a British carrier at sea in 15 years.

After completing SW 21-1, the CSG returned to port to embark fuel and stores for the Fortis cruise. While transiting back to Portsmouth on May 19, *QE* met up with her sister ship, *POW* – which was conducting Fleet Operational Sea Training (FOST) in UK waters - marking the first time they had sailed together. After briefly visiting home, *QE* departed Portsmouth on May 22 to begin her first operational deployment.

Led by *QE*, CSG-21 began its Fortis cruise by participating in two large-scale drills, including the latter stages of the NATO-led Exercise Steadfast Defender 21, which was held off the coast of Portugal from May 20-28. Meanwhile, the F-35Bs took part in the French-led Exercise Atlantic Trident 21 alongside other fighters from the RAF, USAF and French Air and Space Force. Held from May 17-28, the drill aimed to improve the air combat readiness of the three participating nations, while enhancing overall integration at the operational and tactical level. CSG-21 subsequently conducted exercises alongside regional NATO allies in the Mediterranean, including the French Navy's flagship 'flattop', FS *Charles de Gaulle* (R91), during Exercise Gallic Strike 21, a joint training drill held from June 1-3.

The UK cemented the return of its Carrier Strike capabilities on June 20, when 'The Dambusters' conducted the UKLF's first operational strike mission from *QE*. Launched alongside the USMC's F-35Bs, the strikes were carried out in support of Operation Shader – Britain's contribution to wider coalition efforts to defeat ISIS forces in Iraq and Syria. This mission took place almost a decade after the UK's last maritime strike operations over Libya as part of Operation Ellamy in 2011.

After the mission, Cdre Moorhouse said: "To date, we have delivered diplomatic influence on behalf of the UK through a series of exercises and engagements with our partners, now we are ready to deliver the hard punch of maritime-based airpower against a shared enemy."

He said the involvement of *QE* and her air wing in this campaign also "sends a wider message" and continued: "It demonstrates the speed and agility with which a UK-led [CSG] can inject fifth-generation combat power into any operation, anywhere in the world, thereby offering the British government, and our allies, true military and political choice."

Just days after CSG-21 transited through the Suez Canal into the Red Sea on July 6, the

> *"The success of this trial heralds a new dawn in how we conduct maritime aviation and is another exciting step in the evolution of the Royal Navy's [CSG] into a mixed crewed and uncrewed fighting force"*
> Rear Adm James Parkin, the Royal Navy's Director Develop

Multi-mission Merlins

Headquartered at RNAS Culdrose, Cornwall, the Merlin HM2-equipped 820 NAS is responsible for detecting/countering airborne and subsurface threats while deployed with the Carrier Strike Group. For any deployment, the HM2 forms the backbone of rotary-wing operations from the carriers.

Powered by three RTM322 turboshaft engines, the HM2 is equipped with a Selex Galileo Blue Kestrel 5000 maritime surveillance radar and a Folding Light Acoustic System for Helicopters (FLASH) dipping sonar. It can be armed with a mix of Sting Ray acoustic-homing lightweight torpedoes, Mk11 depth charges and a Browning M3M .50-cal machine gun. While primarily used for ASW operations, HM2s can also support search-and-rescue (SAR), casualty evacuation, humanitarian assistance/disaster response (HA/DR), maritime patrol and interdiction missions.

Several Merlin HM2s have been equipped with the Crowsnest ASaC role kit to meet the airborne early warning (AEW) requirements of the UK's new carrier air wing (CVW). A Crowsnest-fitted HM2 is equipped with a Searchwater 2000 radar, providing an early warning of both air/surface threats. The system is housed in an inflatable kevlar bag attached to an arm on the port side of the aircraft's fuselage that is lowered into a vertical position when in use. Two Navy observers utilise the Cerberus tactical sensor suite in the helicopter's cabin to interpret the radar picture and co-ordinate other aircraft during operations.

Crowsnest is a crucial part of the CVW's operational architecture, though it faced several issues during its transition into frontline use. Having been rushed into service to support CSG-21 during Operation Fortis, the system fell below operational expectations and its performance was heavily scrutinised due to instability with the initial System Release 11 software.

To address these issues, improved System Release 11.4 software was delivered to 820 in April 2022, with the update being applied to the ASaC Mission Trainer at Culdrose and on two Merlins deployed with HMS *Prince of Wales* (R09) in May/June, that year. In mid-2022, 820 NAS began flight testing with the new System Release 12 software, which featured better overland surveillance capabilities, an improved ability to communicate with the F-35Bs and new radar modes.

The Navy eventually declared IOC with Crowsnest in July 2023, before deploying the "most advanced version" of the ASaC system on HMS *Queen Elizabeth* (R08) in September that year. CSG-25 will serve as the most significant test for the platform to date, especially as it seeks to attain Full Operational Capability (FOC). Despite this, the UK aims to replace the system with an uncrewed aircraft by 2030, but a seven-year timeframe for this feels optimistic when considering the problems faced during Crowsnest's development.

Moorhouse later told *Sky News*: "In that sort of cat-and-mouse-type game, I am absolutely clear they are turning away at ranges where they are probably using us to facilitate their own training in the same way that we would do towards them. They were not engaging or locking us up or anything like that, but the ranges at which they were flying were indicative of what they would do for real."

On October 3, CSG-21 carried out integrated naval operations in the Philippine Sea with both the US Navy's Ronald Reagan and Carl Vinson CSGs, as well as the Japan Maritime Self-Defense Force's (JMSDF) Hyuga-class helicopter destroyer, JS *Ise* (DDH-182). This drill involved integrated air operations, air-defence scenarios and simulated strikes against naval targets with the aim of strengthening interoperability between the three nations.

After conducting joint drills with the Republic of Korea Navy, CSG-21 began its journey home on October 20. Unfortunately, *QE* experienced her first loss on November 16, when a British F-35B (ZM152/'018') crashed into the Mediterranean while attempting to take off from the carrier. The pilot safely ejected from the jet, which plummeted to the seabed. Following the aircraft's recovery, it was determined that a protective engine intake blank had become stuck down the left intake duct and was almost invisible during pre-flight checks. While the incident was avoidable, it adds to the lessons learned from CSG-21 and will be refined for *POW's* upcoming CSG-25 deployment.

On the prowl

The UK's new carriers can accommodate both the 'Commando' Wildcat AH1s operated by 847 NAS and the Wildcat HMA2s flown by 815 NAS. The former can support UK Commando Helicopter Force (CHF) operations, while the latter typically conducts ASW/ASuW missions while deployed with the UK CSG on operational cruises. The Navy currently fields 28 Wildcat HMA2s from Yeovilton.

While the multi-role maritime helicopters are key to defending the UK CSG from surface/subsurface threats, they would typically deploy aboard the carrier's escort vessels, rather than the 'flattop' itself. Powered by two CTS800-4N turboshaft engines, the HMA2 is fitted with a Seaspray 7400E active electronically scanned array (AESA) multi-mode radar and an MX-15Di electro-optical/infrared (EO/IR) system, which also makes it a potent intelligence, surveillance, target acquisition and reconnaissance (ISTAR) platform.

Fitted with Leonardo's Weapon Wing, the HMA2 can be armed with up to 20 Thales Martlet lightweight air-to-surface missiles or up to four MBDA Sea Venom anti-ship missiles when configured for ASuW operations. For the ASW mission, the Wildcat is capable of using the same weapons as the Merlin HM2 (Sting Ray torpedoes and Mk11 depth charges). The helicopters are also armed with a Browning M3M .50-cal machine gun.

group briefly joined the US Navy's Iwo Jima Amphibious Ready Group (ARG) and Ronald Reagan CSG for drills in the Gulf of Aden. It then carried out several drills with the Indian Navy. CSG-21's arrival in the Indo-Pacific signified the UK's commitment to strengthening diplomatic, economic and security ties with India and other allied nations, promoting the freedom of passage through vital trading routes and open and inclusive order.

Following a scheduled port visit to the British Defence Singapore Support Unit (BDSSU) in Sembawang, Singapore, *QE* and her escorts entered the South China Sea on July 26 to conduct freedom of navigation exercises across the area, despite rising tensions in the region: China claims territorial ownership over Taiwan and the South China Sea, and criticises the presence of foreign warships operating in the area – this was no different for CSG-21.

While in the region, CSG-21 used its ASW assets to detect and track Chinese submarines, allowing *QE* and her escorts to avoid them. The carrier's AEW assets also tracked a number of Chinese warplanes, which operated no closer than approximately 150 miles (241km) from the strike group's position.

Above: **Air Engineering Technicians (AETs) aboard POW prepare to load a training variant of the Sting Ray acoustic-homing lightweight torpedo onto an 820 NAS Merlin HM2 before the ASW helicopter departed the carrier for a mission during Exercise Steadfast Defender 24 on February 28, 2024** *MOD Crown Copyright/LPhot Belinda Alker*

Below: **Equipped with a Leonardo Weapon Wing, this Wildcat HMA2 (ZZ518) from the FAA's 815 NAS conducts the first operational firing of the Thales Martlet lightweight multi-role missile in the Bay of Bengal during the Operation Fortis (CSG-21) deployment on October 16, 2021** *MOD Crown Copyright/ LPhot Unaisi Luke*

Going Commando

Both Queen Elizabeth-class carriers can launch sustained amphibious operations. Alongside the Merlin HM2s, both vessels can also accommodate the 'Commando' Merlin HC4s operated by 845 NAS 'Junglies' from Yeovilton. A vital part of the CHF, this specialist 'Commando' unit is tasked with providing troop transport and load-lifting support to elements of the Royal Marines that deploy with the carriers – namely 42 Commando, which specialises in maritime operations.

Previously operated by the RAF as the Merlin HC3/3A, the fleet was transferred to the FAA in 2012 to support Commando Helicopter Force operations. As part of the Merlin Life Sustainment Programme (MLSP), 25 HC3/3As were upgraded to HC4-standard and equipped with the same cockpit electronics as the HM2, as well as folding tails and main rotor blades, deck lashing mounting points, a strengthened landing gear, fast-roping points, a common emergency egress system and other obsolescence updates. Flight trials began with the HC4 in 2017, with the variant achieving Initial Operational Capability (IOC) in mid-2018.

The carriers are also rated to carry RAF Chinook HC5s and AAC operated Apache AH2s. The former conducted its first landing aboard QE in February 2018, while the latter – which only achieved IOC in May 2023 – has yet to embark. Despite this, the AH2's predecessor, the Apache AH1 was familiar with the warships, after completing three days of Platform Ship Integration Testing (PSIT) to ensure the gunship could be supported by the carrier while deployed.

Together with the 'Commando' Merlins and Wildcats, the Apaches and Chinooks can be used to form a large littoral manoeuvre package, conducting combat missions near the shore in support of amphibious assaults. With such operations, the Navy says that while the carriers do "not have the surface assault capability with landing craft of the specialist ships, [their] four-acre flight deck provides plenty of scope from which to project manpower and equipment ashore using the variety of helicopters [they] will be able to host".

QE returned to Portsmouth on December 9 after seven months at sea, marking the end of the Navy's most significant peacetime cruise in a generation. While deployed, CSG-21 travelled 49,000nm (56,388 miles or 90,748km) and visited more than 40 countries.

The ascending prince

Despite suffering significant flooding in October 2020, which damaged her electrical cabling and forced the vessel to return to dry dock for eight months, *POW* was declared fully operational in October 2021. On January 11, 2022, she assumed the flagship role of NATO's Maritime High Readiness Force from the French Navy. In this role, *POW* was intended to support NATO exercises in the Arctic, Baltic and Mediterranean for a 12-month period.

POW departed Portsmouth on August 27, 2022, for joint drills with allies off the US East Coast. However, on August 29, she suffered major mechanical issues with her starboard propeller shaft, forcing the warship back to dry dock at Rosyth, which took nine months to complete. *QE* replaced *POW* for the US deployment.

After returning from the US, *QE* embarked eight UKLF F-35Bs and seven helicopters before participating in Operation Achillean in the North Sea, which aimed to validate NATO's new fifth-generation strike capabilities. While deployed from September to December 2022, the CSG participated in large-scale military operations, including ASW drills with RAF-operated Poseidon MRA1 maritime patrol aircraft.

On September 8, 2023, *QE* – complete with eight UKLF F-35Bs, five Merlin HM2s (of which, two carried the Crowsnest ASaC system) and three 847 NAS-operated Wildcat AH1s (in their first deployment aboard the carrier) – embarked on her next major cruise: Operation Firedrake. During this, the CSG – comprising *QE*, *Diamond*, *Kent* and *Tideforce* – completed a series of drills in northern European waters with the UK Joint Expeditionary Force (JEF) and other NATO partners.

POW returned to sea for trials on July 21, 2023, after being repaired at Rosyth. While *QE* was engaged in operations associated with Firedrake in September, *POW* began

trials with various UAV systems designed for the resupply mission. Partnering with the UK-based firm, W Autonomous Systems (WAS), these trials sought to evaluate the feasibility of drones delivering up to 220lb (100kg) of supplies to the UK CSG while deployed.

History was made on September 8, when a WAS-designed cargo UAV successfully landed on the deck of *POW* off the Cornish coast, delivering supplies to the 'flattop' before returning to Predannack Airfield, Cornwall. This twin-engine, twin-boom UAV – which is capable of carrying a 220lb (100kg) payload at ranges of up to 621 miles (1,000km) – was the second fixed-wing aircraft type to operate from the Queen Elizabeth-class warships.

After deploying to the US East Coast, *POW* marked another major milestone on November 15, when a General Atomics Aeronautical Systems (GA-ASI)-operated Mojave UAV took off and landed back on the carrier's deck in what was the first trial of its kind. A variant of the MQ-1C Gray Eagle MALE UAV that has been adapted for short

Owned and operated by GA-ASI, this Mojave UAV (N450MV) – a specially modified STOL variant of the MQ-1C Gray Eagle – takes off from the deck of POW during a unique trial off the US East Coast on November 15, 2023. This trial showcased the carrier's ability to operate large, fixed-wing UAVs alongside manned fifth-generation assets
MOD Crown Copyright/LPhot Finn Stainer-Hutchins

take-off and landing (STOL) operations, the drone – being 6m (20ft) wider than an F-35B – was the largest aircraft of its type to be operated from a non-US 'flattop'.

This trial demonstrated how modern, fixed-wing UAVs can be operated alongside crewed assets, such as the F-35B. Rear Adm James Parkin, the Royal Navy's Director Develop, whose team planned the trial, said: "The success of this trial heralds a new dawn in how we conduct maritime aviation and is another exciting step in the evolution of the Royal Navy's [CSG] into a mixed crewed and uncrewed fighting force."

POW embarked on her first major deployment when she participated in Exercise Steadfast Defender 24 – the largest NATO-led exercise to be held since the end of the Cold War – from January to May 2024. Initially, *QE* was scheduled to take part in the drill, but faults with the warship's starboard propeller shaft resulted in her being dry-docked for repairs until July. While operating off the Norwegian coast during Steadfast Defender, *POW* and her CSG participated in the UK-led JW 24-1, before taking part in the Norwegian-led Exercise Nordic Response 24, which culminated with *POW* leading a 15-ship

formation that combined the UK CSG with a NATO Amphibious Task Group. *POW* returned to Portsmouth on March 26.

From October 14-27, *POW* ventured into the North Sea for Exercise Strike Warrior 24, which played a key role in preparing the carrier and her strike group for CSG-25. The drill involved personnel from 809 NAS 'Immortals' and the wider UKLF, marking the first time that an FAA-badged fast-jet squadron had operated from a British 'flattop' in nearly 15 years. Eight F-35Bs joined *POW* for this deployment, allowing 19 pilots to gain their carrier qualifications. During Strike Warrior, F-35Bs flew 71 sorties (totalling 210 flight hours) from *POW* and dropped four Paveway IV laser-guided bombs (LGBs) on the Cape Wrath Training Area in Sutherland, Scotland.

Having concluded Strike Warrior, *POW* is regrouping with the UK CSG to conduct more vital training before the task force embarks on the carrier's first long-term deployment to the Indo-Pacific, scheduled to begin in April. CSG-25 will closely mirror that of CSG-21, but with *POW* leading the fleet.

While details regarding the number of vessels and aircraft that will support this deployment have yet to be publicly released, the mission – which will last for several months – will see the UK CSG participate in a series of exercises/operations while supporting Westminster's goal of strengthening and fostering political and defence relationships with partners in the Far East and demonstrating its commitment to promoting a free and open Indo-Pacific. **afm**

As aircraft maintainers work on the four F-35Bs visible on her flight deck, POW steams through the North Sea during Exercise Strike Warrior 24 on October 24, 2024. This exercise provided an opportunity for the carrier, her air wing and other UK CSG vessels to conduct work-up activities ahead of the global CSG-25 deployment this year
MOD Crown Copyright/POPhot Alex Ceolin

Baltic defenders

Allies continue to safeguard NATO skies as Italy and France take over Baltic Air Policing Block 67 in Lithuania.
Giovanni Colla and **Remo Guidi** report

The last rays of the day's sun illuminate these Italian air force F-2000s over the Baltic skies. They are both equipped with IRIS-T and AIM-120 missiles, plus Litening V pod under the fuselage All images Giovanni Colla and Remo Guidi unless stated

Since its inception in 2004, NATO's Baltic Air Policing mission has been crucial in ensuring the security and sovereignty of the Baltic states' airspace. The mission, now in its 67th rotation, sees Italy and France working side by side to safeguard the skies above Lithuania, Latvia, and Estonia. With operations based at Šiauliai Air Base in Lithuania, this iteration reflects NATO's commitment to collective defence.

Baltic Air Policing was launched as part of NATO's initiative to support the Baltic States following their accession to the Alliance. These countries, lacking advanced air defence capabilities, required the assistance of NATO's more robust air forces. Over the past two decades, 17 Allies have participated in this peacetime defensive mission. Lieutenant General Thorsten Poschwatta, Commander of NATO's Combined Air Operations Centre (CAOC) in Uedem, Germany, emphasised the mission's significance: "For over 20 years, handing over the key to the Baltic Airspace has been the symbol of what this Alliance represents: the

The snow can't stop this F-2000A – the Task Force Air is ready 24/7 to safeguard the Baltic region

Above: **A Typhoon pilot gets ready to start his Typhoon's EJ200 engines**

Right: **A French AF Rafale B assigned to EC 02.004 'La Fayette' taxiing out for a training mission**

strong collective will to defend our shared values and ensure durable cohesion."

Italy: Leading with Eurofighters

Dubbed Task Force Air (TFA) 36th Wing – Operation Baltic Thunder II, the Italian Air Force detachment is equipped with four Eurofighter Typhoon (F-2000) aircraft from the 36th Wing in Gioia del Colle, the 4th Wing in Grosseto, the 37th Wing in Trapani, and the 51st Wing in Istrana alongside E-550A Conformal Airborne Early Warning (CAEW) and Beechcraft Super King Air 350ER SPYDR aircraft assigned to the 14th Wing in Pratica di Mare which have operated from Lithuania only during specific periods.

Italy's deployment took the lead in the 66th rotation at Šiauliai Air Base, Lithuania (August – November 2024), succeeding Portuguese and Spanish detachments in mid-2024. During this four-month rotation, the first Alpha Scramble occurred on August 3, 2024, when NATO's Combined Air Operation Centre at Uedem scrambled two Italian Air Force Eurofighter Typhoons in response to potential threats from Russian military aircraft. The Italians identified two Russian MIG-29s flying over the international waters in the Baltic Sea, close to Alliance territory. The Eurofighters escorted the Russian aircraft, demonstrating the high state of readiness and proficiency of the Italian detachment. Under NATO's Air Policing mission, an Alpha Scramble is triggered when an aircraft is flying an invalid or incorrect flight plan; fails to or loses communication with the relevant air traffic control authority; or fails to communicate with the air traffic control authorities using the transponder, an electronic device that emits a four-digit signal called a squawk code.

After surpassing 1,000 flight hours – including the CAEW and SPYDR aircraft's

flight hours – conducting 32 Alpha Scrambles, and intercepting 48 Russian military aircraft, the mission has been handed over to the next – and current - Italian detachment and their French colleagues forming the 67th rotation. During the formal handover ceremony, which took place on November 28, 2024, and upon receiving the symbolic key to the Baltic Airspace, the incoming commander, Colonel Roberto Massarotto – Commander of the TFA 36th Wing, highlighted the importance of the ceremony as a testament to NATO's core principles and strength. "This key not only symbolises the unity and purpose of NATO but also represents a great responsibility. Rest assured, we will undertake the task of ensuring Baltic Air Policing with the same commitment we apply to protecting our own airspace," he affirmed.

As geopolitical tensions rise due to the ongoing conflict between Russia and Ukraine, NATO's Air Policing missions have evolved significantly, adopting a deter and defend philosophy and Italy has been actively supporting NATO's Air Policing mission along the eastern flank in recent years. In 2024, Italian aircraft operated out of Malbork, Poland, initially deploying F-35s (see *CAJ* February 2024 issue) and later transitioning to Eurofighters (see *AFM* October 2024 issue). With the 67th rotation the Italian air force TFA 36th Wing continues to demonstrate its commitment to collective defence, underscoring the importance of cohesion and solidarity among Allied nations.

The TFA's mission in Lithuania centres on preserving the integrity of Baltic airspace. Continuous surveillance, rapid response, and the interception of unauthorized aircraft

A Rafale crew prepare for a training mission

Above: **French AF detachment commander Major Sanka**

Right: **Col Roberto Massarotto, Task Force Air 36th Wing Commander** *Italian Air Force*

are critical components of their operations. Speaking on the heightened importance of Air Policing, the TFA commander highlighted that the ongoing crisis in Ukraine underscores the need to monitor and defend airspace against unconventional threats. "Being here today symbolizes shared responsibility and solidarity among Allied nations," Massarotto emphasized, noting that the deployment of Eurofighter Typhoons and the advanced E-550A CAEW has significantly bolstered NATO's defensive capabilities.

As for all the previous air policing deployments, Italian Eurofighter Typhoons drawn from various wings across Italy, form the backbone of TFA operations. These aircraft – renowned for their advanced capabilities – are integral to the NATO Air Policing mission. "The Typhoon is Europe's most advanced combat aircraft, constantly evolving with new technologies and armaments," said the commander. Italy's extensive experience with these aircraft has enabled seamless integration and standardization across NATO's air forces. Mixed crews and shared training procedures further enhance interoperability, ensuring that TFA personnel can operate effectively in multinational teams. The Italian Air Force took advantage of the integration within the Task Force Air of the E-555A CAEW (Conformal Airborne Early Warning) into operations, which has marked a new era in NATO's surveillance and battlefield management capabilities. "The CAEW aircraft initially contributed to EVA (Enhanced Vigilance Activity) operations to monitor the airspace over Northern Europe and Iceland and later joined patrol missions in the Baltic States. It is the most advanced multi-sensor system for airborne surveillance, command, control, and communications currently in service among European air forces. The AEW-BM&C (Airborne Early Warning, Battlefield Management & Communication) capability is now an essential tool for ensuring an adequate extension of national airspace surveillance capacity (Homeland Defence/Security)," the commander explained. Its deployment has significantly extended NATO's ability to monitor and secure Baltic airspace, enhancing situational awareness and response times.

Lithuania, as the host nation, provides invaluable civil and military support to NATO forces stationed within its borders. This collaboration extends to joint training exercises that benefit both parties. The TFA commander expressed appreciation for Lithuania's logistical and technical support,

This image epitomises the true meaning of NATO concept 'Stronger together' – two French Rafale B flying side by side with two Italian F-2000A

Italian AF F-2000A leading a four-ship formation composed of two French Rafale B and two Italian F-2000A

which has been instrumental in maintaining 24/7 operational readiness. Joint missions with Lithuanian assets have yielded significant training advantages, fostering mutual skill development and operational integration. "The partnership strengthens NATO's defensive posture while enhancing the

Below: A pair of Italian air force F-2000As. The Italian air force F-2000s will stay in Lithuania until end of March after completing block 66 and block 67 rotation in the Baltic region

Below middle: An opposite break of two Italian AF F-2000s in the Baltic skies

Below right: A close-up shot of two Italian AF F-2000s in a beautiful winter light

professional capabilities of all participants," the commander stated.

NATO's commitment to standardized procedures ensures seamless co-operation among member states in the region. "We participated in several training events, including the NATO operation Neptune Strike 24-2, a series of advanced missions with Swedish colleagues operating the JAS 39 Gripen fighter jets (September 23-25, 2024), co-operation with the Lithuanian navy (ADEX), Close Air Support (CAS) activities in various NATO exercises in the Baltic States, such as exercise Furious Wolf," explained Massarotto. "These joint efforts underline the Alliance's determination to maintain security in a rapidly evolving geopolitical landscape."

During Neptune Strike 24-2 (October 24-31, 2024) Italy, with its Eurofighter Typhoons, played a leading role, significantly contributing to the air component of the operation. Numerous air co-operation activities were conducted in the Baltic Sea region and Eastern Europe, in co-ordination with naval and ground assets. These activities aimed to increase interoperability and standardization through highly realistic training scenarios focused on interception missions. The exercises took place in multinational Joint and Combined environments, involving fighter aircraft and personnel engaged in Air Policing missions or deployed across Europe, including participants from the United States,

Above: A Typhoon pilot poses for a shot at flight level FL100 (10,000ft)

Right: Here's looking at you – Rafale B crews from above at FL100 (10,000ft)

Finland, the United Kingdom, France, and, following its recent NATO accession, Sweden. Neptune Strike was not merely a military training exercise but a tangible demonstration of international co-operation. Armed Forces from various nations came together to refine their capabilities, expressing a strong commitment to reinforcing NATO's security framework in the Baltic states, enhancing allied forces' readiness, deterring aggression, and reaffirming the Alliance's dedication to the defence and protection of all its member states.

A few months before exercise Neptune Strike, the Italian detachment participated in exercise Furious Wolf, held in Estonia, Latvia, and Lithuania from August 19 to September 6, involving NATO countries in close air support manoeuvres. This exercise was a demonstration of international co-operation, bringing together armed forces from various nations to refine their capabilities. Specifically, air and ground forces had to co-ordinate precisely to manage diverse and often complex tactical situations in scenarios where air power supports and operates in symbiosis with land operations. During numerous sorties, air-to-air refuelling activities were also conducted with multinational assets, including the Airbus A330 MRTT aircraft. From air defence to intelligence, reconnaissance, surveillance, and air-to-ground attacks, the Eurofighters, as multirole Swing Role fighters, demonstrated their broad operational capabilities in the exercise scenarios. Italy concluded the exercise with over 40 flight hours across approximately 30 day and night sorties.

Since August, and at the time of *AFM*'s visit to Lithuania (early December 2024), the TFA has flown over 1,000 hours and conducted 300 sorties, including several dozen Alpha Scrambles to intercept and identify unauthorised aircraft. These missions have not only ensured airspace integrity but have also served as valuable training opportunities. "The experience gained through joint exercises and real-world operations has enhanced our crews' capabilities, preparing them for any scenario," the commander stated. Training missions blend air-to-air (A/A) and air-to-ground (A/G) exercises, with Lithuania's dedicated ranges enabling simulated armament deployments.

Looking to the future, the TFA commander emphasized the importance of continuing joint exercises and building on the operational successes achieved thus far. The integration of advanced technologies, such as the Litening V targeting pod for extended identification and tracking capabilities, further strengthens NATO's defensive framework. "We use the Litening V on all aircraft as a mission enhanced because it has the ability in the air-to-air profile to identify aircraft at long distances. Once the target aircraft is locked on using the radar or IRST, we can track it with the POD. With its cameras, we can observe the details of the intercepted aircraft without being detected, maintaining adequate distances," Massarotto explained.

France: Rafales to enhance the mission

From December 1, 2024, four French Air Force Rafale B from Escadron de Chasse 2/4 'La Fayette' – Saint Dizier Air Base – augmented the Italian Eurofighters in Lithuania, providing NATO with an effective Air Policing capability. France had participated in NATO Air Policing in the Baltic region since 2007; this deployment marked the third consecutive year that the French Air and Space Force has deployed to the region. Mirage 2000-5 aircraft were stationed there in 2023, and Rafale C jets were deployed in 2022. "It was a great pleasure for us to participate in this collective mission as a NATO nation," said Major 'Sanka', French Rafale Detachment Commander. "The integrity of the Baltic Sea area was important for European sovereignty, which is why France had been contributing regularly to its protection," he added.

The additional second detachment at Šiauliai allowed for more flexible operational planning of NATO Air Policing in the region. Deployed allies benefited from additional opportunities to conduct training with other regional air, ground, naval, and special forces, as well as practice Agile Combat Employments, further enhancing the skills, interoperability, and

An opposite break of two Italian air force F-2000As

resilience of our air forces. Over the next four months (until the end of March), the mission will be divided into 'hot' and 'cold' weeks. During 'hot' weeks, the French jets will maintain operational readiness, prepared to intercept any suspicious or unannounced flights near the airspace of the Baltic nations. In 'cold' weeks, the focus will shift to operational preparation, although the Rafale jets will remain on standby for potential real-world alerts if their allies face issues.

Renowned for its technological maturity, the Rafale has become more and more a crucial player in air policing. "The Rafale is a state-of-the-art aircraft with cutting-edge technology," Sanka said. "It allows us to achieve better performance, track targets from greater distances, and integrate easily into tactical networks. The ability to share information with allied forces makes the pilot's and crew's jobs easier and more efficient." The Rafale fleet includes both single-seater and twin-seater variants, each serving distinct roles. The twin-seater version at his first appearance for an Air Policing mission offers greater flexibility, allowing pilots to conduct both air-to-air and air-to-ground operations simultaneously. "The twin-seater model allows us to perform multiple tasks at the same time, such as air-to-air and air-to-ground missions. It's an extremely versatile platform for a wide range of missions," said Sanka.

International co-operation is at the heart of air policing missions and Sanka emphasised that while operational approaches among NATO nations are largely aligned, communication remains a critical challenge. "During the early stages of the Ukraine crisis in 2022, differences in communication protocols between countries made it difficult to co-ordinate efforts effectively. We had some difficulties communicating with other nations because we didn't always share the same communication protocols. But over time, we have developed a better understanding, and now it's much easier to work together."

The training and co-ordination between nations are also vital components of air policing success. The French Air Force works closely with the Italian Air Force, ensuring that both forces are fully prepared to operate together in the Baltic region. "We are working closely with the Italians, and we make sure that both teams train together, so when it's time to conduct operations, everyone is on the same page," said Sanka. A careful balance of 'hot' and 'cold' training periods allows both teams to train alongside one another, ensuring that all personnel, regardless of nationality, are ready to work as a unified force when the need arises.

Since this is the first Air Policing mission for the Rafale B, logistics played a pivotal role in the successful execution of air policing missions. Sanka explained that the French Air Force has learned valuable lessons from previous deployments, especially when it comes to integrating mission operations and communication systems. "Deploying large numbers of personnel and aircraft to foreign locations requires meticulous planning and co-ordination. The integration of mission operations and communication was a challenge at first," he said. "When we first deployed here, we didn't have the best methods for communicating with NATO forces. But over time, we've developed more efficient and secure communication systems, which has made a huge difference in the success of our missions."

By maintaining a strong presence in the region – like Italy – France demonstrates its dedication to NATO's collective defence principles and reaffirms its role as a key player in the alliance's defence strategy. "For France, air policing in the Baltic is essential. It's about European security, and it's important for us to show that we are committed to these issues. We are here every year, ensuring that we uphold our national mission while contributing to NATO's collective security," Sanka emphasized. The four Rafale B from Saint Dizier were due to be replaced at the end of January by four Rafale from BA118 Mont-de-Marsan which were due to stay until the end of 67th rotation – at the end of March 2025. **afm**

Italian AF F-2000A leading a four-ship formation composed of two French Rafale B and two Italian F-2000A

GLOBAL AUTHORITY ON MODERN MILITARY AVIATION, DELIVERING EXCLUSIVE NEWS AND UNMATCHED COVERAGE

At *AirForces Monthly* we are at the cutting edge of modern military aviation and every month we bring you the latest news, analysis, and features that you won't find anywhere else.

Each issue of the magazine is packed full of exclusive content and detailed briefings by our team of experts and our legion of correspondents from across the world.

Don't miss out on this great subscription offer!

Alan

Alan Warnes, Editor at Large

SUBSCRIBE TODAY!

WHICH OFFER WILL YOU CHOOSE?

OFFER 1 - GOOD!
£62.99 — SAVING £8.89!
12 issues (£5.25 an issue!)
PLUS A **FREE GIFT**
Paying by Credit/Debit Card

OFFER 2 - BETTER!
£29.00 — SAVING £6.94!
6 issues (£4.83 an issue!)
PLUS A **FREE GIFT**
Paying by 6 month Direct Debit

OFFER 3 - BEST!
£56.99 — SAVING £14.89!
12 issues (ONLY £4.75 an issue!)
PLUS A **FREE GIFT**
Paying by Annual Direct Debit

REASONS TO SUBSCRIBE...
» **SAVE** over buying individual issues
» **SUBSCRIBER DISCOUNTS** on *Key Publishing* event tickets
» **EXCLUSIVE** Subscriber offers on the *Key Publishing* Shop
» **DELIVERED DIRECT** to your door
» BE THE FIRST to read the latest features

SCAN THE QR CODE TO ORDER DIRECT FROM OUR SHOP
shop.keypublishing.com/afmsubs
or call **+44 (0)1780 480404** *(Lines open 9.00-5.30, Monday-Friday GMT)*

DOING IT THE FRENCH WAY

As it does every year, the French Air and Space Force launched a **Pégase** mission in April 2025, this time in Europe, pending a possible larger-scale deployment elsewhere next year. **Henri-Pierre Grolleau** reports

A mixed formation comprising a Rafale B and a Polish F-16D Fighting Falcon above the Polish countryside near Poznań during Pégase 2025 All photos, author

An F-16C and a Rafale C share the ramp at Poznań Air Base

Pégase missions have become the signature of the French Air and Space Force (FASF) long-distance projections. They are the subject of careful preparation: "The route for Pégase 2025 was finalised at the beginning of 2025," explained General Patrice Hugret, Commander of the Pégase 2025 mission. "We are now opting for a long-distance deployment in even-numbered years, and a shorter mission in odd-numbered years. Our goal is to strengthen our relationships with key partners and achieve various effects. During the preparation phase, we carefully studied the detachment format, destinations, routes, and desired effects, including the strategic signal and demonstration of our capability to act swiftly and reassure our partners. All of this is the subject of dialogue, reflection, and analysis between the French Chief of Air and Space Staff, the FASF's Air Defence and Air Operations Command, the FASF's HQ, including its International Relations Office, and the various units involved. We also consider operational readiness and training objectives for our personnel. From there, we generate resources while maintaining the right balance between what we commit to Pégase and what we retain, in France or elsewhere, so as not to penalise other operational missions and the daily organic training of the squadrons."

Desired effects

For the Pégase 2025 mission, three countries were selected for the deployment of the FASF force: Sweden, Poland, and Croatia. "The international context lends itself to this choice, with the deployment being divided between Northern Europe, Central-Eastern Europe, and the Balkans," General Hugret continued. "We are therefore covering an immense area in nine days, stretching from the Far North to the Adriatic Sea. It is a true demonstration of our operational expertise and an exciting expeditionary mode, derived from the NATO concept known as ACE or agile combat employment. Applicable to all areas of the world, it is a concept in which we excel because we rely on our internationally recognised expertise in the fields of planning, operations, and logistics."

Several objectives were set for Pégase 2025:
• Reassure the countries on Europe's eastern flank and demonstrate France's determination to participate in the defence of European interests in the broadest sense, by rapidly mounting a force and power projection operation for their benefit, with an AWACS, in-flight refuelling tankers, and multiple fighter jets, all supported by a logistical chain between France and the forward bases.
• Strengthen partnerships with allied countries. For example, Pégase 2025 represented the third deployment of French military aircraft in Sweden this year, following the deployment of an MRTT tanker and then Rafale fighters, which engaged in air policing and air defence operations in the Baltic countries. Poland, a country that heavily invests in its defence and that of Europe, was also chosen by French decision-makers to strengthen ties with its airmen by improving mutual understanding. This effort coincided with Pégase 2025, which took place just days before the meeting between President Emmanuel Macron and Polish Prime Minister Donald Tusk in Nancy. Finally, Croatia belongs to the Rafale community, and its air force continues to build up its fleet of the French twin-engine jet.
• Discourage bad intentions with a non-escalatory conventional deployment, by demonstrating, as was done during Pégase, the ability to support French elements pre-positioned in the Baltic states as part of the Lynx/eFP (enhanced forward presence) mission at a moment's notice.
• Demonstrate the latest FASF aircraft in action, under real-life operating conditions, to prove that they are agile, robust, reliable, and easy to operate daily. This effort focused in particular on the A330 MRTT Phénix and the A400M Atlas.

Very long-range raid

Pégase Grand Nord (Far North) began with a very long-range raid, including live firings of laser-guided bombs at a Swedish firing range. This ambitious operation required extensive preparation in close co-operation with foreign partners to obtain all the necessary authorisations for overflights of friendly countries by aircraft equipped with war-ready weapons.

For the first phase of Pégase 2025, the FASF had mobilised significant resources: an E-3F AWACS, three A330 MRTT Phénix tankers, one A400M Atlas airlifter, six Rafale B/C fighters (four two-seaters from Saint-Dizier and one single-seater and one two-seater from Mont-de-Marsan, all F4.1 standard), and three Mirage 2000D RMV strike fighters, which operated independently of the rest of the force. "On April 22, we conducted a long-distance raid from France," explained Colonel Clément Amagat, deputy operations officer for Pégase 2025. "Each aircraft departed from its home base, and the entire force,

> *"The weather was marginal, but the two bombers managed to deliver a live GBU-12 each on the Lomben firing range, near the town of Kalix, with both targets illuminated by Swedish special forces."*

Colonel Clément Amagat talks to a French Rafale pilot just after the detachment landed in Croatia

French Rafales and Polish Fighting Falcons flew advanced combat training missions during Pégase 2025 to hone their respective fighting skills. Contrary to what has been posted by other media, the Rafales did not simulate nuclear missions

"Everywhere, we received a fantastic welcome, which helped strengthen strong, friendly relations."

except the A400M, regrouped above the Bay of Somme before heading towards the North Sea. It was there that a Royal Air Force A330 MRTT refuelled our fighters in bomber configuration. Indeed, two of the Rafales from Saint-Dizier were each armed with four GBU-12 laser-guided bombs, two with live bomb bodies and two with inert bomb bodies, hence the need to obtain diplomatic clearances to fly over the countries concerned. They were heavier and dragged more than the unarmed Rafales, hence the need to call on the British Voyager to supplement our three Phénixes,

one of which also refuelled our AWACS. The force then transited via Denmark, then via the south and east of Sweden, flying over the Baltic Sea before entering Swedish airspace defended by four Gripens armed with Meteor missiles. The raid was then reduced to a single Phénix, the AWACS, and the six Rafales. The two fighters from Mont-de-Marsan fulfilled the sweep mission ahead of the raid while their counterparts from Saint-Dizier assumed the striker function. Our two 30th Escadre de Chasse Rafales also had to protect our high-value assets, the AWACS and the last Phénix.

The weather was marginal, but the two bombers managed to deliver a live GBU-12 each on the Lomben firing range, near the town of Kalix, with both targets illuminated by Swedish special forces. Direct hits were recorded. These were the first live weapons firings directly from France as part of a power projection training event. This long-distance operation is thus similar to the raid conducted in 2013 in Mali from Saint-Dizier. This is the result of great multinational co-operation with our British and Swedish friends. Two points that I would like to emphasise in this presentation: the AWACS

A Croatian Rafale EC and a French Rafale B sit on the ramp at Zagreb

Général Patrice Hugret, Commander of the Pégase 2025 mission. He flew Rafale Marine while detached to the French Navy and later commanded a Rafale squadron

directly retransmitted its L16 image to the Lyon Mont-Verdun command centre thanks to the Joint Range Extension system, while the Phénix, with General Hugret and me on board, acted as a flying command post."

At the end of this raid, the Rafales and the Phénix landed at the Luleå base, home to the F21 wing and its JAS-39C/D Gripen fighters. The three Mirage 2000Ds extended their route to Finland, where they continued their mission alongside the local F/A-18C/D Hornets without interacting with the rest of the Pégase participants. At the same time, the AWACS returned directly to Avord.

Multi-Axis Co-operation

Following this initial highlight, Pégase 2025 facilitated numerous interactions with multiple partners in the northern and eastern regions of Europe, as well as in the Balkans. "The flights continued at a particularly sustained pace throughout the mission," emphasised Amagat. "The following day, our Rafales fired two additional GBU-12s at Lomben for the benefit of Swedish forward air controllers. With and against the Gripens, advanced long-range and short-range combat scenarios were practised, making full use of their immense training area, including very low altitude/very high-speed flights at 300ft and up to 550kts. The Phénix and the A400M refuelled the Gripens, thus demonstrating full Franco-Swedish interoperability. To enhance the scenarios and vary the partners, our pilots also worked with Finnish F/A-18C/Ds. On Saturday, April 26, three of the Rafales from the 4th Escadre de Chasse returned to Saint-Dizier via Estonia, where they simulated ground attacks in co-operation with allied forward air controllers of the NATO multinational battalion. The other three Rafales and the A400M left Luleå for Poznań Air Base in Poland, bypassing the Russian enclave of Kaliningrad, while the Phénix landed at Poznań International Airport. In addition to missions with Polish F-16s, our Rafales trained with Royal Air Force Typhoons temporarily stationed in Malbork, Poland. On Tuesday, April 29, our Rafales carried out a mission as part of the NATO Neptune Strike exercise in the Mediterranean, directly from Poznań before landing in Zagreb. Finally, our interaction with our Croatian comrades was highly beneficial to both parties, marked by a joint flight on Wednesday, June 30, and the first in-flight refuelling of a Croatian Rafale by a Phénix on the same day. Everywhere, we received a fantastic welcome, which helped strengthen strong, friendly relations."

Complex missions

Pégase 2025 allowed Rafale crews to conduct integrated operations with Swedish JAS-39C/D Gripens, Polish F-16C/D Fighting Falcons, and Croatian Rafale EC/DCs. Captain Anthony, an EC 1/4 'Gascogne' pilot, agreed to describe some of the flights

French and Croatian aircrews pose at the end of their joint missions. The Croatian pilots have kept their helmets on to hide their faces.

A French WSO salutes while taxiing out for an air-combat training exercise.

"Even though it is less powerful, the Gripen is ultimately quite comparable to the Rafale."

he took part in: "In Sweden, I participated in an Offensive Counter-Air mission during which the Rafales of our patrol played a swing role, simulating an attack on buildings and hangars using simulated AASM guided munitions. The Gripens and two additional Rafales escorted us. We shared data with them on the same L16 network at the BU2 standard, for Block Upgrade 2, the most advanced iteration of the Link 16. A huge area was reserved for us, the largest I have flown in since the beginning of my career. It is at least four times larger than TSA 43, the largest of the French air combat training areas, above the Massif Central. It is a mixed civil and military airspace, but with very little civilian traffic. Their air traffic controllers proved excellent at segregating civilian and military aircraft. Even though the Gripens and two other Rafales were conducting a sweep 20nm ahead of us, we also ensured our self-protection thanks to the Rafale's formidable air-to-air capabilities. To reduce our vulnerability, we descended to a low altitude for a high-speed, very low-altitude penetration. The many lakes were still frozen, and there was snow everywhere. A superb landscape! In front of us, eight Gripens representing the Red Air Force were trying to block our passage. My navigator and I constantly kept an eye on the tactical situation, a mix of L16 tracks and tracks from our own RBE2 AESA radar. Thanks to this, we avoided threats and delivered our weapons in a simulated manner."

Defending a NATO meeting

From Poznań, FASF airmen collaborated closely with their counterparts in the Polish Air Force, conducting particularly complex air combat missions that followed elaborate scenarios. "In Poland, I was engaged in a Defensive Counter-Air mission during which we had to defend a simulated NATO leaders' summit against an enemy raid aimed at disrupting, or even preventing it," Captain Anthony explained. "Two of our Rafales were engaged, including mine, with the Polish Air Force's Second-in-Command in the rear seat. The friendly Blue Air force consisted of eight F-16s and our two Rafales, while the aggressor party had six Red Air F-16s. To ensure the defence of the meeting, two Front Combat Air Patrols, each composed of four F-16s, were facing the enemy on two lanes [parallel tracks] West/East. At the same time, a Rear CAP with a Rafale was responsible for engaging any hostile leakers who might have managed to pass or bypass the defensive curtain of the Blue Air F-16s. My Rafale was kept at a distance to demonstrate the aircraft's capabilities to the Polish general while monitoring the progress of the fight via the L16. Unfortunately, the Rafales and the F-16s were not on the same L16 network because the Polish F-16s are still equipped with the earlier L16 Block Upgrade 1. Polish fighter controllers performed an excellent job of targeting by assigning each enemy aircraft to a friendly fighter, thereby avoiding overkills, i.e. the firing of several missiles at the same target by multiple aircraft. Equally importantly, they ensured that each hostile was targeted to guarantee that no leaker would manage to reach the NATO meeting. Polish pilots are very professional. They are accustomed to NATO-type exercises and operate in a manner very similar to ours. The Polish Mission Commander of the Blue Air Force led the fight as we would have done. This is very reassuring, and it demonstrates our ability to

At Poznań Air Base, A400Ms, F-16s, and Rafales were closely guarded by heavily armed Polish force-protection specialists

carry out joint missions without any difficulty thanks to procedures shared by all."

With the Croatian Rafales

Croatia has acquired a total of 12 ex-FASF Rafales, comprising ten Rafale C single-seaters and two Rafale B two-seaters, which are now respectively designated Rafale EC and DC in Dassault Aviation's official export terminology. For Pégase 2025, the FASF had decided to deploy three of its Rafales to Croatia to strengthen the mutual relationship and participate in a joint air-to-air mission. The welcome given by the Croatian airmen to their French counterparts at the Zagreb base was particularly warm, with the crews of both nations taking the opportunity to strengthen the already close ties established in mainland France during the Croatian airmen's conversion onto the Rafale.

"We conducted a joint two-v-two mission, with two mixed patrols, each consisting of a Croatian single-seat Rafale EC and a French two-seat Rafale B," Captain Anthony explained. "As in Poland and Sweden, the briefing was face-to-face, which allowed us to clarify each other's intentions and needs, and to increase the fluidity of the mission. We were not part of the L16 network with our Croatian comrades, but the two French Rafales were in L16 formation with each other for security reasons during take-offs, positioning, and return phases. On the other hand, as we were playing against each other in mixed patrols, the L16 was cut off as soon as we entered combat. Although they are still in the process of appropriating the

Dogfights

In addition to complex, massive missions, one-on-one close-quarters combats were organised in Sweden and Poland to train pilots for all scenarios, including those where the aircraft would merge in a dogfight, after an inconclusive long-range engagement. For these flights, Rafale configurations were quickly adapted, with the 2,000-litre wing tanks being removed and smaller 1,250-litre drop tanks being installed under the central pylon.

Captain Anthony shared his impressions of these close-quarters combats against a Gripen, an F-16, and a Typhoon: "Even though it is less powerful, the Gripen is ultimately quite comparable to the Rafale," he said. "Like the Rafale, it is comfortable at low speeds due to its canard/delta wing aerodynamic formula, which is quite like that of the French aircraft. However, due to its lower engine thrust, it degrades its energy more quickly in combat. The F-16 is much more powerful than the Gripen. However, it is also an older-generation aircraft, as it has less nose authority than the Rafale, which means its pilot will be less comfortable at high angles of attack. He will therefore have more difficulty turning very short and pointing the nose of his aircraft towards his opponent for a gunshot. I also had the chance to do a dogfight against a Typhoon, but I came across a young pilot, and it quickly went very badly for him."

Pegase Grand North patch

Croatian Air Force Rafale patch

aircraft and ramping up their Rafale tactics, I think that our Croatian friends demonstrated excellent air-to-air tactical skills."

The Pégase 2025 mission once again demonstrated the maturity, flexibility, and power of the FASF's Rafale/Phénix/Atlas package. The ability to 'bounce back' extremely quickly from one base to another while conducting simulated combat operations was also proven, with the ACE concept validated from foreign military installations with a light logistical footprint. Few air forces in the world are capable of conducting operations like these at such a sustained pace, and it is thanks to the advanced expertise and professionalism of its entire personnel that the FASF can organise these deployments. **afm**

This A400M, configured as a tanker with an underwing pod, was used to refuel Swedish Gripens

The Luftwaffe's last two Tornado Wings, TaktLwG 51 and TaktLwG 33, operate in the SEAD and nuclear/precision ground attack roles Gary Stray

Riding
the whirlwind

The Tornado was the Luftwaffe's most numerous aircraft from the early 1980s. Today, just two wings remain, and they are due to be phased out by 2030. **Kevin Wright** talks with Tornado aircrew from both units

Germany purchased 357 Tornados in the early 1980s; fewer than 85 remain in service, fulfilling two crucial roles. Tactical Air Wing 51 (TaktLwG 51) 'Immelmann' operates from Jagel-Schleswig Air Base in Schleswig-Holstein. It flies in the Electronic Combat Reconnaissance (ECR) role, a long-standing euphemism for the highly specialised Suppression of Enemy Air Defence (SEAD) task. Büchel Air Base and temporarily its current operating base at Nörvenich – is home to the Luftwaffe's

Tactical Air Wing 33 (TaktLwG 33). It maintains aircraft on nuclear alert, as the Luftwaffe's direct contribution to NATO's nuclear forces.

SAM suppressors

The Luftwaffe ordered 35 ECR Tornados in 1986. Their cannon armament was deleted, and they were fitted with the more powerful RB199 Mk 105 engines. The first was delivered in May 1990, with the final example handed over on January 28, 1992. It was also the

last of 357 Tornados assembled by MBB at Manching for the Bundeswehr.

The aircraft is operated by TaktLwG 51 'Immelmann' at Jagel Air Base, having assumed the ECR role from JBG 32 in 2013. The unit controls all the Luftwaffe's ECR Tornados, plus a small number of the original IDS versions and some dual-control 'GTs' trainers.

Lt 'Daniel' (full name withheld) is a weapons systems operator with TaktLwG 51 who joined the wing in 2022 and described its aircraft and their critical task. The heart of the Tornado

Two ECR Tornados from TaktLwG 51 'Immelmann' return to their home base at Jagel-Schleswig.
Bundeswehr/ Florian Friz

ECR is its Texas Instruments Emitter Location System (ELS). He said: "Our role is to find, fix and attack enemy air defences, suppressing them to protect our attack aircraft as they approach their targets. After major updates, our Tornados are pretty much state-of-the-art for locating enemy air defence systems.

"We try to sequence our activities so that enemy systems remain out of operation for as long as our bombers could potentially be vulnerable to them and requires precise co-ordination with the attack aircraft. We mainly operate between 8,000ft and 24,000ft because of local airspace restrictions in Europe, but our sensors and the HARMs work well at these altitudes. We also practise at low-level, where the Tornado operates at its best and where it is safest for us when in contested airspace. In an actual conflict, we would prefer to fly very low.

"The ECR can carry up to four AGM-88 HARM missiles, but two are more usual, which allows us to carry extra fuel tanks. For self-defence, the aircraft has a wing-mounted BOZ Chaff/Flare dispenser. A Tornado Self-Protection Jammer (TSPJ) is carried to provide electronic countermeasures."

He continued: "We would not necessarily have to launch our HARMs during wartime missions to be successful. We are also successful if we force the enemy to shut down their radars and air defences through our presence, effectively suppressing them for a few hours while our attack aircraft pass through their threat ring. In the SEAD role, we closely co-ordinate with our attack formation to know their time on target and the direction they will approach so we can maximise our protective cover for them.

"We locate the enemy's SAM systems using our Tornado's ELS. We can then attack them with our AGM-88 HARM missiles, GBU-54s or unguided bombs, either destroying the enemy systems or at least forcing them to shut down to avoid being hit. Our attack aircraft can safely enter the enemy threat ring to hit their designated targets. We can also 'bait' the enemy systems with our aircraft, but that is a very high-risk tactic and not something we usually do."

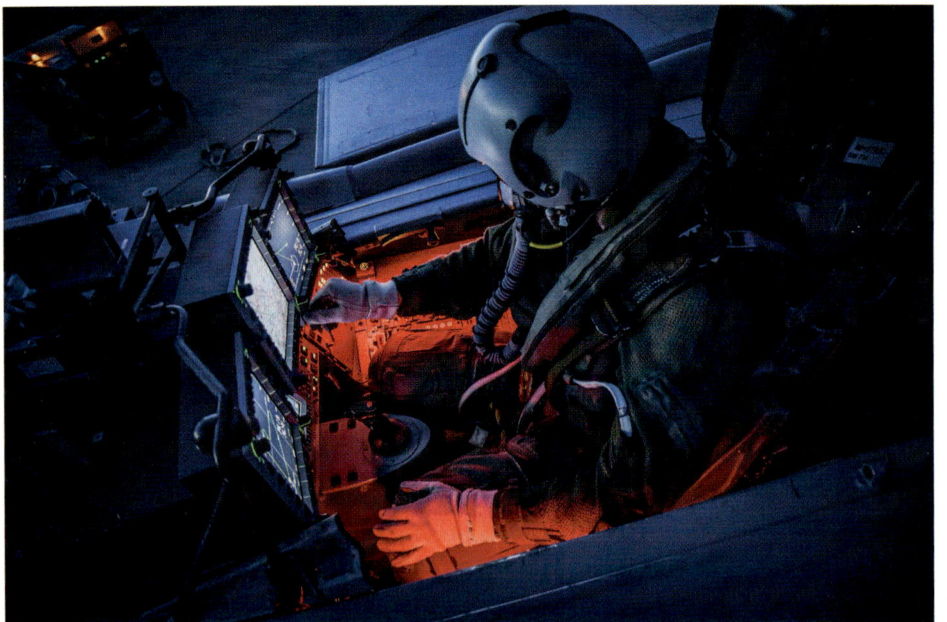

Upgrades

Lt Col 'Chris' (full name withheld) is a Tornado navigator and current CO at the Luftwaffe's TaktLwG 33 at Büchel. From 2013 onwards, a series of 'ASSTA' updates modified the aircraft's software and hardware. Col Chris described the upgrade TaktLwG 33 Tornados have undergone: "ASSTA 3.0 brought a Multi-functional Information Distribution System (MIDS)/Link 16 to improve crew situational awareness and interoperability, plus a secure anti-jam UHF radio. Even without full functionality at that stage, Link 16's importance in improving the crew's situational awareness cannot be overestimated. It also brought better displays for the navigator and a new screen

*Left: **ASSTA 3.1 was a major mid-life update for Luftwaffe Tornados, including new multi-colour displays for the WSOs** Bundeswehr/Oliver Pieper*

*Below and top: **In 2024, TaktLwG 51 hosted the NATO Tiger Meet and painted an aircraft to mark the event** Bundeswehr/Celina Nestler*

for the pilot. Soon after, we got ASSTA 3.1, another significant mid-life update that brought full functionality to the Link 16. We are now up to ASSTA 4.1, with all our jets getting this recent software update, which has brought even more improvements. We feel this gives us capabilities up with the Eurofighter.

"ASSTA 3.0 enabled us to carry the 230kg (500lb) GBU-54, LJDAM (Laser Joint Direct Attack Munition), which has become our main weapon. With a relatively small warhead, it is great for precision interdiction and close air support. We can use it in GPS mode or by lasing the target, selecting the impact angles and different bomb fuse settings. We still have stocks of dumb bombs, but have not trained in using them very much since we obtained the precision GBU-54 capability. It was a huge leap forward for us. Before that, we had the GBU-24, another laser-designated weapon, a 910kg (2,000lbs) bomb, a bunker buster, or a wide area weapon depending on the warhead option chosen.

"We also have the Taurus air-launched cruise missile. It is an important weapon because it gives us considerable standoff capability. Our Tornados carry two 27mm Mauser cannons, each with 180 rounds, mainly used for ground strafing attacks. We carry two IRIS-T missiles for self-defence, a great short-range air-to-air weapon."

Strike/attack

Col Chris added: "When I came to the squadron, we did mostly medium-level conventional operations, as we used to do in Kosovo and Afghanistan. In the last two years, there has been a shift in emphasis back to low-level flying. We practised this in our recent large Pacific Skies exercise in Alaska. While we never lost the capability to operate at low level, there is a renewed importance attached to the techniques used.

"We are working hard with the GBU-54, using it as a GPS weapon. We can set the impact angle and use it in a lofted delivery, allowing us to stand off a considerable distance from the target. We are also using the lofted release in conjunction with laser designation. You come in very low, climb, release the bomb and laser mark the target. It is tough to do when you are pulling up from an extremely low level, but we are getting into it."

TaktLwG 33's Tornados are also Germany's contribution to NATO's nuclear deterrence forces. The Luftwaffe is one of several NATO air forces that commit dual-capable aircraft, like the Tornado, F-16 and increasingly the F-35A, to the Alliance's nuclear forces. Col Chris explained: "The nuclear role is still our top priority. That comes first, we must ensure we are always ready for that, all our other conventional mission capabilities are second to it."

Replacement

While the Tornado has given excellent service, it is facing imminent replacement. Col Chris said: "The Tornado's airframe was intended to operate with us for around 3,000 hours over 20 years. Some of our jets have flown more than 6,000 hours and some will fly for over 40 years before they are retired. The avionics are great after the MLUs, but the airframe is getting old.

Pacific Skies 24

In June 2024, TaktLwG 33 deployed 12 Tornados to Alaska as part of Exercise Pacific Skies 24, a major international event involving US, French and Spanish aircraft. As Lt Col Chris, CO of TaktLwG 33 'Ghost' Staffel, explained: "Our Tornados' involvement was limited to just the Alaskan phase. Our Eurofighter and tanker elements later continued to Hawaii, Australia, India, Japan and New Zealand. The Joint Pacific Alaska Range Complex covers an area equivalent to a large part of Germany. For us, it was superb to fly at 100ft in reheat and know that we were disturbing no one, as the entire area is almost completely uninhabited.

"This was an all-in scenario for Büchel. Most of the wing's aircrew, from both Staffels, ground crews and support staff, were involved. It was unusual for us to deploy on a large scale from just one wing. Pacific Skies was a big commitment; we left just a few crews back in Germany. It was great for both squadrons to work together again, especially as we have had to split up our operations while temporarily operating from Nörvenich.

"During the first two weeks, we focused on low-level flying. At home, we can normally fly down to 500ft, but in Alaska, we stepped down to 100ft, which initially took some practise to become accustomed to. We got to drop GBU-24 and GBU-54 weapons on the ranges, too. It was great to do more operationally realistic tactical flying training than we can do back in Germany."

A TaktLwG 51 Tornado departs Joint Base Elmendorf-Richardson, Alaska, on a training mission during Pacific Skies 24 USAF/SRA Julia Lebens

TaktLwG 33 Tornados are able to operate at night, in bad weather, at low level and over great distances with precision-guided and nuclear weapons *Kevin Wright*

Take off from Nellis AFB during a Green Flag West. TaktLwG 33 Tornados can mount precision attacks with targeting pod and GBU-24 Paveway bombs Bundeswehr/Johannes Heyn

Things break, and having been built by three countries, who all used different subcontractors, many of whom are no longer in business, it is getting harder to get some spares items."

After early expectations that Germany might purchase F/A-18E/Fs and EA-18Gs to meet its Tornado replacement needs, the Luftwaffe settled on a mix of Eurofighters and F-35As to fulfil the ECR and nuclear roles. After the German government gave the go-ahead on November 29, 2023, Airbus confirmed that it would develop a dedicated SEAD variant of the Typhoon, dubbed Eurofighter *Elektronischer Kampf* (EK). The initial purchase is for 15 'Step1' aircraft to be NATO-certified by 2030. Built from retrofitted Tranche 2, 3 and 4 aircraft and equipped with a Saab Arexis ELS and AGM-88E Advanced Anti-Radiation Guided Missiles, they will replace the Tornado ECR.

Commander of the Luftwaffe's Air Forces Command Lt Gen Günter Katz has declared that the Luftwaffe is already considering a 'Step 2' enhancement programme to "further enhance the Eurofighter's electronic warfare capability". He added: "Our vision ranges from escort jammer pods to man-unmanned teaming (MUM-T) solutions, which are currently being worked out in co-operation with our industry partners."

Nuclear mission

Two recent factors are impacting TaktLwG 33's continuing nuclear mission. The US has recently introduced an updated version of its veteran B-61 nuclear weapon, in service since 1967, the new B61-12. This device has a lower yield than its predecessors and can be delivered in ballistic or guided modes.

The new weapon has undergone a re-certification process to ensure the B61-12 can be safely carried by the dual-capable aircraft that could be required to use it: the F-15E, F-16 (MLU), F-35A and German

*Above: **A test shape B61-12, underneath a WTD 61 Tornado at Edwards AFB in September 2024** Task Force 23*

*Left: **Maj Gen Derek France, HQ USAFE, in a HAS at Büchel AB where the 7501st Munition Support Squadron has custody of the B61 nuclear bombs stored there for TaktLwG 33's alert Tornados** USAF/ SRA Jovante Johnson*

Service life extension

A substantial service life extension programme on the Tornado intended to keep the aircraft airborne until 2030 is being undertaken at the Airbus plant at Manching. For example, having accumulated 5,400 flight hours, TaktLwG 33 Tornado 43+42 was approaching permanent grounding. In addition to flying from Büchel, it had operated from Holloman AFB in the USA for several years, training Luftwaffe Tornado crews.

On May 24, 2017, it was flown to Manching to the Airbus Defence and Space site with its hangar space for 20 Tornados. Once there, the external wing tanks and pylons were removed, the aircraft's paint was stripped and the airframe was checked for external damage. Six Luftwaffe personnel and 14 Airbus employees dismantled almost the entire aircraft. They checked the condition of the Tornado's structural components and refurbished and replaced parts where necessary. Once the aircraft was rebuilt, it returned to Büchel in March 2021 and is now cleared for up to 8,000 flight hours and expected to remain in service until the intended 2030 out-of-service date.

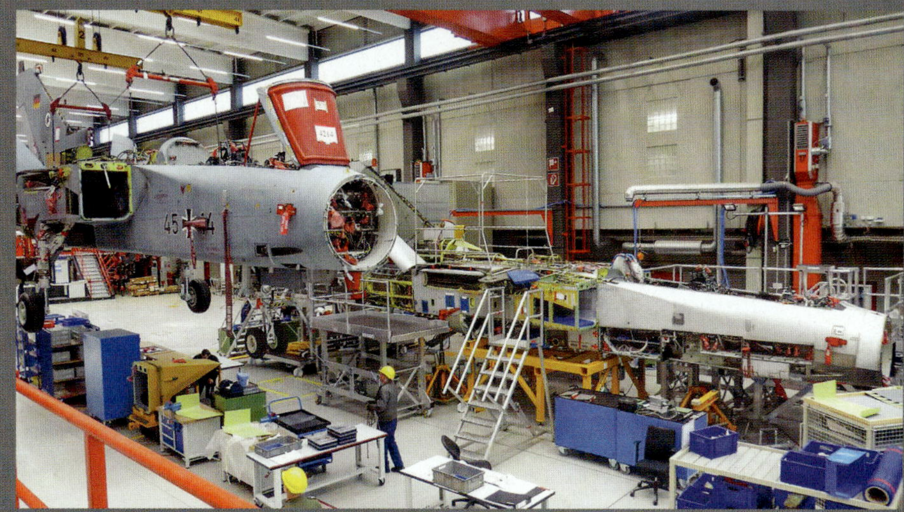

At the Manching plant, electrical wiring is ongoing on one aircraft, while Tornado 45+14 is prepared for structural work Airbus

Tornado. At least one German Tornado has been spotted in the US trialling test shapes of the new weapon.

In December 2022, Germany contracted for 35 F-35As to replace the Tornado in the nuclear role. The possibility of purchasing more aircraft is under consideration, with a further eight frequently mentioned during the summer of 2024. Announced as the most cost-effective solution, with many other NATO member states purchasing the F-35A, it offers economies of scale and substantial operational commonalities. US authorities publicly disclosed the clearance for the F-35A to carry the B61-12 in March 2024.

Work to allow the smooth introduction of the F-35A in Luftwaffe service at Büchel is already well under way and necessitated a

Below: A TaktLwG 33 Tornado is pushed back into a shelter at Nörvenich. From June 2022, the base has become the wing's temporary home, while major reconstruction work takes place at Büchel in preparation for the arrival of the F-35A Bundeswehr/Andreas Zeitler

temporary move for TaktLwG 33's Tornados, as Col Chris explained: "There is major ongoing construction work here. The runway is being completely rebuilt, taxiways resurfaced and improvements to the base's lighting and domestic infrastructure are being made. As a result, we temporarily ceased flying from there in 2022, transferring operations to the Eurofighter base at Nörvenich, about an hour's drive away. We expect to return to full operations from Büchel in 2026.

"We plan on operating Tornados until the F-35A arrives from 2027 onwards. Because we hold a nuclear role, we cannot gradually reduce Tornado operations as we approach the out-of-service date. We will maintain the capability to fully meet our nuclear commitments until a final date is fixed when the F-35s will take over those responsibilities. Our challenge is maintaining our Tornados' fully operational status until that date." **afm**

Mildenhall
matters

It's been a busy year at RAF Mildenhall as **Bob Archer** reveals

RC-135U 64-14847 is shown landing at Mildenhall on October 26 while making one of the type's regular European visits All photos, author unless stated

Royal Australian Air Force KC-30A, A39-004, arrives at Midlenhall on April 6, delivering special forces personnel to exercise with the resident 352nd SOW

RAF Mildenhall has been one of the most exciting air bases for visitor activity in recent times and 2024 was no exception. A wide variety of aircraft transited the base, quite aside from those performing the usual transportation roles. The rarest was undoubtedly the Botswana Lockheed C-130H and the most unusual were a pair of Boeing EA-18G Growlers.

Mildenhall is located in a sleepy backwater of eastern England, but the facility is anything but lethargic. While not supporting the same high volume of traffic as Ramstein, Germany, Mildenhall continues to be an important base for the USAF in Europe and Air Forces Africa, as well as a primary US aerial refueling air station. Airlifters often quick-turn at Mildenhall on their flights to their final destination, with one such a 15th Wing C-17A 05-5152 based at Hickam AFB, Joint Base Pearl Harbor-Hickham, Hawaii, which landed on November 10, and planned to depart to Ramstein after a brief refueling for both aircraft and crew. However, due to a flying control malfunction, which required prolonged repairs, the crew returned home by others means. Once the issues were rectified a replacement crew was organised, who arrived at Midlenhall and who finally flew the aircraft away on December 3.

The 100th Air Refueling Wing remains the host unit ay Mildenhall, which continues to function with a complement of 17 Boeing KC-135R and T models of the Stratotanker. However, the wing usually only has 15 in residence at any one time, as two are regularly away in the US on major overhauls. In previous years, the wing would have received a pooled replacement aircraft prior to sending one of their own for planned depot maintenance (PDM) with the Oklahoma City Air Logistics Center (OC ALC) at Tinker AFB. The system has now changed whereby the 100th ARW has a core number of aircraft, so when an 100th ARW aircraft completes PDM it is returned to Mildenhall ahead of the next one beginning overhaul.

The year 2024 was the 90th anniversary of the RAF station officially being opened. This milestone was commemorated by the unveiling of new station crest, the Tudor Crown, used by King Charles III, replacing the St. Edward's Crown formerly used by Elizabeth II. The new design is being applied to the tails of all 100th ARW KC-135 Stratotankers.

Operations by the 100th ARW were largely unchanged from previous years, with the unit having the primary role of providing aerial refueling training for USA fighter squadrons in Europe, as well as aircraft from other NATO air arms. The 100th also regularly supports the RC-135s that rotate to Mildenhall with the 95th Reconnaissance Squadron. Most RC missions from Midlenhall do not require aerial refueling, but more lengthy sorties, such as those to the Barents Sea or to Ukraine, are always provided with at least one tanker to extend the period on station.

Occasionally, aerial refueling support is provided for fighter aircraft performing patrols of NATO's eastern border with Russia and Belarus. However, the Copper Arrow rotation of reservist KC-135s to Powidz Air Base, Poland, which began in March 2023, when the commitment moved from Spangdahlem AB, Germany, has relieved some of this commitment from the 100th. The unit also assists Air Mobility Command (AMC) or reservist tankers with long distance fighter aircraft deployments. These can be either transatlantic or those staging through the UK while flying to or from the Middle East.

AC-130J 16-5846 landing at Mildenhall on April 2 displays a 30mm cannon and 105mm howitzer protruding from the port side. The array of sensors which acquire targets as well as the defensive antennae are also clearly visible Andrew McKelvey

Above: *436th Air Mobility Wing Lockheed C-5M Galaxy 86-0021 parked on the cargo ramp at Mildenhall on April 6. Note the colourful DOVER tail stripe, as well as second tail band containing 'Super Galaxy'*

Collectively, the 100th launches KC-135s every day of the week, often assuming an early morning departure by multi-point refueling system configured aircraft, compatible with hose and drogue receivers. Whereas for many years the station was closed at certain times during the night and at weekends, Mildenhall now has a 24-hour capability. Likewise, the resident KC-135s frequently perform sorties on days when the station is closed to all but essential movements.

Visiting Tankers
KC-10A
For four decades the McDonnell KC-10A Extender was a regular Mildenhall visitor, but these have gradually been reduced and they are now all retired. The last multiple visit was by a trio of 60th Air Mobility Wing KC-10As – 84-0191, 86-0027 and 86-0031 – supporting the movement of 14 492nd FS F-15Es to the US on February 26 and 28. A small number of single visits followed, until the final KC-10A flight from Mildenhall by 86-0031 departed on August 12 to support four USAF F-16Cs which were returning to the US following overhaul by SABCA at Charleroi, Belgium. More than 40 years of service by the Extender was completed at Mildenhall with the same lack of fanfare as when the first example, 79-0434, visited the base on May 30, 1981. Nicknamed *Big Sexy* due to its alluring sleek wing design and *Gucci* because the KC-10As was cool, excellent and good looking, it bowed out on September 26 in a small ceremony at Travis AFB, California.

KC-46A
The Boeing KC-46A established itself as the new tanker supporting transatlantic deployments, as well as conducting the occasional general airlift. The Pegasus visited in small numbers during the first seven months of 2024, with seven arriving in the space of 90 minutes on August 6, supporting a dozen F-22As on a direct flight from Elmendorf AFB, Alaska to nearby RAF Lakenheath. Other KC-46s visited Mildenhall to perform local sorties allowing US crews the opportunity to be familiarise themselves with European operations flown within the changeable UK weather.

KC-135
Mildenhall has continued to host KC-135s in transit between their home stations and locations in the Middle East and Africa. The majority of these were single AMC aircraft, whereas those from the reservist squadrons often came as a quartet. These transit KC-135s have been far less in number than previous years, primarily due to a reduction in US assets in the Middle East. However,

Below: *The 352nd SOW played host to a number of overseas air arms special forces visits, including the French C-130H 5116 that flew sorties to RAF Sculthorpe in mid-April* Andrew McKelvey

the recent expansion in the number of fighter aircraft deployed to the US Central Command region, along with the addition of strategic bombers, has seen a corresponding increase in the tanker fleet to support them. These include a small number of KC-46s, but primarily KC-135s.

Arguably the rarest visitor to Mildenhall for many years, Botswana Defence Force C-130H began its delivery flight at Alverca, Portugal. The aircraft was flown in on May 20 for its official transfer of ownership

During the spring of 2023, a trio of Special Operations Aircraft (SOAR) KC-135s night-stopped at Mildenhall on their flight from McConnell AFB, Kansas, to the US Navy complex at Camp Lemonnier, Djibouti. The aircraft returned to the US some months later. An identical situation took place on April 29-30, 2024, involving SOAR KC-135Rs 58-0011 and 58-0018, which are fitted with Air Refueling Receiver (ARR) systems mounted above the cockpit, as well as conventional SOAR KC-135R 62-3534 and KC-135T 58-0061, all assigned to the

Extremely colourful Rafale C No.146 landing at Mildenhall on June 2 at the completion of its solo display routine at Duxford

Eight US Marine Corps aircraft from the USS Wasp refuelled at Mildenhall on June 9 while flying from the ship to Sweden Andrew McKelvey

22nd ARW. The four are part of the Special Operations Division at McConnell AFB. One returned home in June and another in August, possibly having been replaced in Africa by other SOAR tankers.

Air Combat Command reconnaissance operations

The resident 95th Reconnaissance Squadron has no aircraft of its own but continues to fly a single RC-135V or W Rivet Joint deployed from the 55th Wing at Offutt AFB, Nebraska. The open-ended commitment to maintain an intelligence, surveillance and reconnaissance (ISR) duty in Europe has gained even more importance since Russia invaded Ukraine in 2022. The primary obligation is to regularly monitor frequencies and activities in Russia and Belarus, as well as occupied areas of Ukraine. Sorties are launched at least three times each week as the unpredictability of the Vladimir Putin regime requires the 95th to repeatedly scrutinise communications and determine any changes to the order of battle of Russia and Belarus to ensure both nations do not have any expansion aspirations into NATO territory.

At the beginning of the year, RC-135W 62-4134 was the sole deployed aircraft, which was exchanged for RC-135V 64-14841 on March 9. Additionally, one of the two RC-135U Combat Sent aircraft ordinarily visit the 95th twice each year. They perform their unique tasking of verifying and

Above: **Having spent an extended period between Lakenheath and Mildenhall over the summer and autumn, the Boeing delivery/test pilots occasionally performed some impressive routines with the Qatari F-15QAs** Andrew McKelvey

Below: **One of seven KC-46As that landed at Midlenhall in the space of 90 minutes on August 7 supporting the deployment of a dozen F-22As flying from Elmendorf AFB, Alaska to the Middle East**

updating all manner of known emitters, to acquire the location, capability and other vital data on radars and weapon systems previously unknown. In 2024, 64-14847

arrived on August 18 and was scheduled to return home on September 23, but due to the evolving threats the crew was required to instead fly a monitoring mission, then return to Mildenhall. Subsequently, this aircraft has regularly flown the familiar route over Poland to circumnavigate Kaliningrad, as well as observing and updating the military posture and government communications in Belarus. It finally returned home on November 1. This was one of the longest periods of temporary duty at Mildenhall by a Combat Sent for decades.

Above: The final KC-10A 86-0031 departed Mildenhall on August 12 to rendezvous with four F-16Cs during their flight back to the US Andrew McKelvey

Below: The elongated refueling probe and host of antennas are clearly visible additions to MH-47G 19-02914, seen taxiing at Mildenhall on September 6

Special Operations Command activities

The 352nd Special Operations Wing (SOW) began the year with Bell Boeing CV-22Bs Ospreys grounded following the crash of a USAF airframe in Japan in late November 2023. However, by April 15, the circumstances of the loss had progressed sufficiently for a CV-22 to undertake ground taxiing. On June 16, 08-0050 flew two very brief air tests, before making a short flight to RAF Sculthorpe the following day. The MC-130Js were largely unaffected by the Osprey grounding, apart from being unable to aerial refuel CV-22s, and being restricted to performing missions solo.

The 352nd SOW fleet remained constant at nine CV-22Bs and seven MC-130Js. While the Ospreys were restricted to operations within the vicinity of East Anglia, the MC-130Js were able to fly training sorties within the UK and conduct exercises in mainland Europe. The wing was host to a number of Air Force Special Operations Command (AFSOC) aircraft in transit between the US, the Middle East and east Africa. US-based AC-130Js and MC-130Js were periodic visitors, some singlys, although on April 2, three 1st SOW AC-130Js night-stopped before departing east. A further two arrived on September 24, but with the serials on the nose and tail taped over. The previous day saw three MC-130Js arrive, looking equally anonymous. All five were eastbound and departed quickly after refueling, except for one of the MC-130Js which was delayed due to a technical issue.

As the year came to a close, there was clearly an increase of AFSOC assets in the Middle East and East Africa. On November 17, a pair of AC-130Js and three MC-130Js all arrived, following the now familiar trend of having their serials obscured. This anonymity is presumed to be a temporary feature, otherwise the serials would have been completely removed, as is the case with AMC aircraft. However, the purpose is likely to be for operational security reasons.

On the evening of November 20, Feltwell, Lakenheath and Mildenhall were each targeted by a number of small unidentified drones. Subsequently, more evening activity was detected in the vicinity of each base, with various authorities being mobilised, including the East Anglian police helicopter, launched in a vain attempt to track and trace the source. Other military activity involved ground elements from the Royal Air Force Regiment at RAF Honington, other branches of the military security services; various police drone experts, as well as the RAF Beechcraft Shadow R1s of 14 Squadron at Waddington. Additionally, Lakenheath F-15Es were launched to overfly the drones and respond to any aggressive activity taking place.

On December 4, AFSOC Dornier C-146A 10-3077 of the 524th SOS arrived for assignment to the 352nd SOW, with the USAF stating that the deployment had been planned since March 2024. A local mission to Sculthorpe was flown the following day to enable the crew to familiarise themselves with operations in the UK.

The wing hosted special forces from other air arms, including the French Air Force, which flew local sorties to Sculthorpe from a C-130H between April 14 -26. Hungarian special forces regularly train with the 352nd, arriving and departing aboard their Airbus A319. Australian Air Force Special Forces also visited between April 6-15, arriving aboard Airbus KC-30A A39-004. The most recent special forces exercise hosted by the 352nd was on October 28-31, when personnel from Hungary were joined by troops from Belgium and France. The latter two air arms brought an Airbus A400 each, which flew day and night sorties to Sculthorpe.

Although unconnected with the 352nd, two highly modified US Army Boeing MH-47G Chinooks, serials 19-02914 and 19-02918, belonging to the 160th Special Operations Aviation Regiment (Airborne) were air-freighted from Hunter Army Airfield in Georgia aboard a pair of Boeing C-17As on September 3. After reassembly and air testing, they were escorted to RAF Odiham by an RAF Chinook HC6A on September 9, enjoying the opportunity to fly low level above the Thames along the designated helicopter lane. They subsequently participated in Exercise Dark Lightning in northern England, before returning to Mildenhall on September 28. After

Above: F-16C 87-0350 was one of eight F-16s from the 555th FS at Aviano AB, Italy, that arrived on September 6 for Exercise Cobra Warrior

Right: The port side tail of 87-0350, which was involved in both Operation Bolo and Rolling Thunder in Vietnam.

RAF Mildenhall based aircraft

As of 08/11/2024

351st ARS KC-135R/T

Key * = Multi-point Refueling System; ** = KC-135T; # = Block 45 Cockpit Upgrade

Serial	Name
57-2605	Wolff Pack
58-0095 **	Silver Dollar
58-0100 #	100 Proof
58-0125**#	The Reluctant Dragon
59-1464**#	Sly Fox
59-1470**	Skipper III
59-1475 #	The Savage
59-1511*	Squawkin Hawk
60-0324	Miss Irish
60-0333*	High Life
60-0335 **	NKAWTG Biggasbird at Tinker for rework
60-0353	Rosie's Riveters at Tinker for rework
60-0355*	Black Jack
61-0315 #	Our Gal Sal
62-3540 #	Holy Terror
63-8878 #	Boss Lady
63-8008*	All American Girl

352 SOW 7 SOS CV-22B

Serial	Name
08-0048	
08-0049	
08-0050	
09-0042	Executioner
10-0053	Perdiem Queen
11-0057	Sir Poppington
11-0058	
11-0061	
16-0076	

352 SOW 67 SOS MC-130J

Serial	Name
09-6207	Boreas
12-5759	War Pig - In USA for checks
13-5776	Independence
13-5778	Night Watcher
16-5839	No name - In USA for repainting
20-5937	No name
20-5941	Judgementer

being dismantled, they returned home in the same manner as they arrived.

US Navy and Marine Corps

In recent years, US Navy visitors have been extremely thin on the ground, although there was a brief refueling stop by Boeing P-8A Poseidon 170015 of VP-30 on October 10 with a partially over-painted tail code 'LL'. The Poseidon was fitted with a Raytheon APS-154 advanced airborne sensor mounted in a slim elongated pod along the underside. This sensor can detect, classify and track targets on land and sea simultaneously. The P-8 was on a flight from NAS Sigonella to Keflavik.

P-8 visitors are relatively infrequent, as those on temporary duty at NAS Sigonella, Sicily, and NS Keflavik, Iceland, rarely need to stop in the UK while in transit between the two facilities. Furthermore, two US Navy P-8s are also located at RAF Lossiemouth to conduct their core tasking of maritime patrol whenever nuclear submarines sail in or out of Holy Loch in the river Clyde. Invariably, Russian vessels are in international waters off the Scottish coast.

Remaining with the larger Navy types, the Lockheed EP-3E Aires II version of the Orion has been an occasional visitor for decades. However, the type is in the twilight of its career, as the ISR role is being taken over by the Northrop Grumman MQ-4C Triton unmanned aerial vehicle. Nevertheless VQ-1 'World Watchers' EP-3E 161410 has been involved in monitoring the ongoing conflict between Israel and groups located in Gaza and southern Lebanon. Sorties were staged from Souda Bay, Crete, until October 30, when the EP-3E flew to Mildenhall before attempting to depart next day to the USA, ahead of returning to NAS Whidbey Island, Washington state. Fog delayed the departure, which was followed by a technical issue, with 161410 finally leaving for NAS Patuxent River, Maryland, on November 1.

The second EP-3E at Souda Bay, 159893 was due to follow via Mildenhall but instead routed through NAS Rota, Spain, on November 2, arriving at Whidbey Island on November 6. These were the final operational sorties by the aircraft before being retired and VQ-1 is due to be disbanded on March 31, 2025. In place of the EP-3Es, the US Navy has already begun using the MQ-4C, with169660 flying above the eastern Mediterranean early on November 2 (the Triton is assigned to Unmanned Patrol Squadron 19 operating from NAS Sigonella).

A shortage of fuel resulted in two Grumman EA-18G Growlers and four Boeing FA-18 Hornets diverting to Mildenhall on October 17. The contingent was from the CVN 75/USS *Harry S Truman*, which was sailing in the North Sea ahead of participating in exercise Neptune Strike 24-2. The six aircraft from Carrier Air Wing-1 (CVW-1) tail code 'AB' were airborne from the aircraft carrier when the vessel sailed too far for their safe recovery. The jets comprised VFA-11 F/A-18F 166640/'104', 166669/'106'; VFA-143 F/A-18E 168922/'202', 166905/'205', and VAQ-144 EA-18G 166931/'500' and 168934/'503'. After approximately four hours at Mildenhall, the aircraft returned to the ship. This was the first occasion that an operational Growler had landed at a military base in the UK. Of these, 166931 was decorated with colourful markings for the commander of CVW-1. One month later, on November 17, MH-60S 167821/'612' also coded 'AB' of HSC-11 made a 90-minute stopover.

Earlier, on June 9, a similar diversion involved eight US Marine Corps aircraft briefly visiting Mildenhall for fuel while they were embarked on LHD 1/USS *Wasp*. They departed the aircraft carrier after training with French special forces. The aircraft were on

A small number of P-8As visited Mildenhall in 2024, with 170015 of VP-30 on October 10 with the APS-154 advanced airborne sensor mounted beneath the fuselage Andrew McKelvey

AC-130J 19-5926 departs Mildenhall on October 6, displaying its firepower protruding from the port side Andrew McKelvey

their way to Ronneby Airport, Sweden, for Baltic Operations (BALTOPS) 24. The first to arrive were four McDonnell Douglas AV-8B Harrier IIs of VMA-365 (Rein) wearing tail code 'YM' serials 164554/'51', 165425/'52', 165580/'54' and 166288/'56', which remained for 90 minutes. As they were departing, four MV-22Bs of VMM-365 also tail coded 'YM' arrived, serialled 168337/04, 168645/06, 168325/10, and 168225/11. The Ospreys stayed for about two-and-a-half hours before continuing to their final destination.

Other Navy visitors included the occasional C-130 transport, although with no naval air facility in residence, there is a much reduced resupply requirement in the UK. Additionally, US Marine Corps KC-130Js visited Mildenhall to clear customs when positioning from their home stations to Teversham Airport, Cambridge, for major overhaul by Marshall Aerospace.

Visitors

Arguably the rarest aircraft to visit Mildenhall during the year was Botswana Defence Force Lockheed C-130H serial OM4, which arrived from Alverca, Portugal, on May 20, following a lengthy period of storage. Formerly USAF serial 74-1675, the aircraft was supplied to the Afghan Air Force in September 2013, but was repossessed by the USA when the Taliban assumed power in the country in 2021. OGMA at Alverca stored the Hercules prior to refurbishing it under the USAF's Excess Defense Articles programme. The gifted aircraft was on its delivery flight from Portugal to Botswana, with the circuitous route being necessary as the official transfer of ownership from the US to the new customer was required to take place at a US military air base.

On January 4, the 430th Expeditionary Electronic Communications Squadron (ECS)

VAQ-144 EA-18G 166931 was one of six jets from CVN 75/USS Harry S Truman which diverted to Mildenhall to refuel on October 17 *Andrew McKelvey*

Bombardier E-11A serial 11-9001 departed Riyadh for the US, with a refueling stop at Mildenhall. These military Global Express aircraft are not uncommon, but the routing from Saudi Arabia to the UK, as presented on ADSB, was extremely interesting, as the flight was shown to have tracked over Simferopol in Ukraine before resuming a conventional course to Mildenhall. It would have been impossible for a sophisticated USAF command and control asset to traverse Russian territory during the present conflict, so why the tracking showed this route is a mystery.

Although Exercise Cobra Warrior 24-1 in the spring was cancelled, Mildenhall hosted fighter aircraft for CW 24-2. It played host again to USAFE fighter aircraft with eight 31st FW F-16Cs of the 555th FS from Aviano AB, Italy, arriving on September 6. The exercise did not begin until September 16, with the preceding week allowing crews to familiarise themselves with northern Europe's congested airspace. The three-week exercise was divided into two weeks of daytime flying and a third devoted to evening/night operations.

The tail art on F-16C 87-0350 was particularly interesting, being a black and pale yellow design with red stars. On the port side was the legend 'Operation Bolo', while 'Rolling Thunder' was inscribed on the starboard. The seven red stars on the tail signified the number of North Vietnamese Mikoyan MiG-21s shot down by McDonnell F-4C Phantoms on January 2, 1967 , during Operation Bolo (named after an agricultural machete that doubles as a Filipino weapon).

A small deployment of four F-16Cs of the 119th FS, 177th FW New Jersey ANG flew from Atlantic City to Aviano for Operation Pegasus Dawn on October 18-25. The operation was designed as an agile combat employment (ACE) training mission to assist the 108th Wing's transition from the KC-135 to the KC-46A. At the completion of the operation, the F-16s flew to Mildenhall, where they remained overnight before flying home the next day. Despite the 108th Wing converting to the KC-46, the flight home was supported by a pair of 305th AMW KC-46s; although it is possible they were crewed by New Jersey ANG personnel.

Overseas visitors at Mildenhall are considerably less common than they were a decade or two ago. A French Air Force Casa

F-16C 87-0230 of the 119th FS New Jersey ANG is shown landing at Mildenhall on October 25 *Andrew McKelvey*

Despite being more than 80 years old, A-26C N26BP performed a very impressive departure after a short stay on June 26 Andrew McKelvey

CN235M delivered ground crew on May 29, to support a pair of Dassault Rafales. One of the pair, 146, was the 2024 Rafale Solo display aircraft and was resplendent in a very colourful red, white and blue design. The aircraft was temporarily at Mildenhall for Duxford's May airshow. The technicians were collected on June 3 by a Luftwaffe C-130J-30, making the maiden appearance by a German Hercules at Mildenhall. The Australian KC-30A mentioned earlier was not the only Antipodean visitor this year, as a C-17A arrived on July 14, possibly to deliver cargo for the USAF.

Two Qatari F-15QAs were delivered from the US to Lakenheath on July 10, followed by two more to Mildenhall on July 13. These four then bounced between Lakenheath and Mildenhall to enable them to participate at the Farnborough and Fairford airshows, before continuing their journey to Qatar some weeks later. A straggler from the October delivery remained at Lakenheath and was still there at the end of the year.

AMC movements

AMC traffic changed little compared to previous years. Boeing C-17s were the most common airlifter to visit Mildenhall, along with the occasional Lockheed C-5M Galaxy, although the latter numbered less than 30 throughout the year. Of these, 87-0030 on July 24 brought Army Air Corps AH-64Es ZM738, ZM739 and ZM740 as airfreight, followed on October 7 by 84-0061 containing ZM741, ZM742 and ZM743. In both instances, the dismantled Apache helicopters were towed to a hangar, where they were inspected and loaded onto trailers for the road journey to RAF Wattisham.

A small number of AMC aircraft were devoid of all markings and serial numbers. This policy was introduced by the previous AMC commander for operational security reasons and has been a gradual process that appears to be continuing, although there has not been any announcement since the new commander took office in September 2024.

Return of reciprocating engines

Civilian traffic at Mildenhall is usually confined to larger Airbus and Boeing airliners ferrying personnel and cargo from the US. However, on June 28, Douglas A-26C Invader N26BP/41-39359 *Million Airess* owned by Marine Aviation Museum Inc arrived while flying in for various UK airshows, including Fairford and Duxford. The highly polished, natural metal Invader had earlier flown over Normandy during the 80th anniversary of D-Day in early June. After a very sporty departure, the A-26 returned to Duxford before flying to Wick Airport in Scotland and Reykjavik in Iceland on the lengthy journey back to Houston, Texas. **afm**

The final visit by an EP-3E to Mildenhall was on October 30 when 161410 arrived from Souda Bay, Crete and departed next day for the US Andrew McKelvey

the Chasing
golden Phantom

The Turkish Air Force celebrated the 50th anniversary of its F-4 Phantoms in November. Cem Dogut looks back at this iconic aircraft's history in Turkish service and shares photos from the celebratory flying events

The Phantom has been flying with the Turkish flag in the skies of Anatolia for 50 years All images Cem Dogut

By the 1960s, the striking power of the Türk Hava Kuvvetleri (Turkish Air Force – TurAF) was formed by the F-84 Thunderstreak and F-100 Super Saber aircraft, which were acquired through the US assistance program. In addition to these, the TurAF was also operating a small number of F-5 Freedom Fighter and F-104 Starfighter aircraft. Due to the problems that began in Cyprus in 1960 and the crisis that escalated with Greece after the intervention on the island in 1964, the need for a new multi-role fighter plane emerged in the early 1970s.

The acquisition of 36 F-4E Phantom IIs by Greece under the Peace Icarus project in 1971, highlighted the necessity of meeting the modern and powerful aircraft need of the TurAF. Contract negotiations with the USA started in February 1972 and were completed in a short time, and the Peace Diamond project was launched within the same year. A total of 40 F-4E Phantom II aircraft were ordered and the project was financed from the national budget.

With the arrival of two F-4E Phantom II (73-1016 and 73-1017) aircraft to the 1. Ana Jet Üs Komutanlığı (1. Main Jet Base Command) with US pilots on August 30, 1974, the Phantom page was officially opened in the history book of Turkish aviation, and the incoming Phantoms entered service with the 113 'Tayfun' Filo (113th 'Typhoon' Squadron), established the same year at Eskişehir. F-4Es were taken to the Turkish skies for the first time by Tayfun Squadron Commander Major Ergin Celasin and Captain Ziya Alemdar with the Phantom 73-1016 on September 2, 1974. Squadron personnel became combat-ready in mid-1975. With the introduction of F-4E Phantom IIs, the Weapon Systems Officer (WSO) class, which did not exist in the Turkish Air Force, was introduced and 'Şimşek' ('Lightning') Air Wing, which was established under the Squadron in 1976, began the combat readiness training of the F-4E Phantom II WSOs. Eight F-4E Phantoms, delivered in 1974, were assigned to the 113 Filo. Of the 32 aircraft that were

The character of Spook, found across the global Phantom community, appears on the belly of F-4E 77-0303 in its red and black anniversary scheme

delivered in 1975, 12 were assigned to the 113 Filo, and the remaining 20 were assigned to the 112 'Şeytan' Filo (112nd 'Devil' Squadron). As part of the Peace Diamond II project, 32 F-4E Phantom II and eight RF-4E Phantom II aircraft were ordered in total. An interesting feature of the Peace Diamond II project is that the 5,000th serial production F-4E was delivered to the Turkish Air Force with the tail number 77-0290 within the scope of this project. The 172 'Şahin' Filo (172nd 'Falcon' Squadron) and the 111 'Panter' Filo (111th 'Panther' Squadron) were modernised with the aircraft that had been purchased since April 1978 under the Peace Diamond II Project.

As part of the Peace Diamond III project, 15 F-4E Phantom II aircraft were supplied from the Aircraft Maintenance and Regeneration Centre (AMARC) in the USA from July 1981

to April 1984. These planes, which were purchased under the Peace Diamond III project, were assigned to the 173 'Şafak' Filo (173 'Dawn' Squadron) after being painted in Southeast Asia (SEA) camouflage.

Within the scope of the Peace Diamond IV project, 15 ex-USAF F-4E aircraft were purchased between 1984 and 1985 to replace the losses of the four Phantom squadrons. These planes were followed by 40 ex-USAF Aircraft F-4E Phantom II aircraft with Peace Diamond V project in 1987. These aircraft were first modernised in the 131 'Ejder' Filo (131 'Dragon' Squadron) and later in the 132 'Hançer' Filo (132 'Dagger' Squadron) at 3rd Main Jet Base Command in Konya.

In 1991, military aid was received from the USA and its allies as a result of the support given to Operation Desert Storm, launched by the US-led coalition to remove Iraq from

Kuwait. In this context, as part of the Peace Diamond VI project, 40 ex-US Air National Guard Aircraft F-4E aircraft were received between 1991-1992.

Innovations for the Phantoms

Phantoms brought about radical changes in the TurAF as a new generation aircraft. A good command of English was required for the documents (Standard Operating Procedure – SOP, Flight Manual etc) used in training in both the USA and in Turkey. This was given great importance in the training. The most difficult thing for the pilots assigned to the F-4 was that the aircraft was operated by two crew. Pilots who had flown in a single-seater fighter aircraft for many years had difficulty adapting to the fact that there was someone else behind them in the rear cockpit. The F-4 had a specific division of labour where the pilot in front was

Phantoms fly over Lake Burdur. The surface of the lake appears golden in colour, appropriate for the aircraft's golden anniversary

Phantoms in a three-ship formation – it was a challenge to maintain formation while flying at low speed for photographers on the ramp

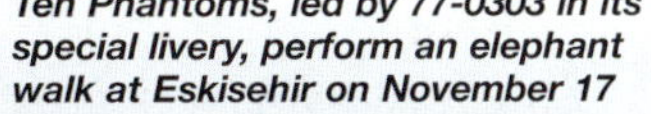

Ten Phantoms, led by 77-0303 in its special livery, perform an elephant walk at Eskisehir on November 17

responsible for flying the aircraft and the WSO in the back was responsible for using the weapon systems.

With the delivery of F-4E Phantom II aircraft, modern munitions such as TV-guided AGM-65A/B Maverick air-to-ground missiles (AGM), AN/AVQ-23 Pave Spike laser targeting pods, laser-guided 500 and 2000lb GBU-10/12 Paveway I/II and electro-optical guided 2000lb GBU-8 HOBOS bombs were also added to the TurAF inventory. In this way, the Turkish Air Force gained the precision strike capability against air-ground targets for the first time in its history.

In addition to these modern munitions, medium-range semi-active radar homing AIM-7E Sparrow and short-range infrared heat-seeking AIM-9B/P Sidewinder missiles began to be used for air-to-air missions. Furthermore, one of the most effective

The Phantom's special markings are revealed in full as it moves away from the A400M by banking to the right

At the start of the Gulf crisis, Turkish Phantoms received air refueling training from American tankers. The first air refueling with an F-4E after the Turkish Air Force acquired the KC-135R aircraft took place on September 20, 1995

The huge red and white Turkish flag on black also resembles the air force roundel

Golden anniversary

There is a special bond between aviation enthusiasts and the Phantom in Turkey, as well as all over the world. It is a concept that connects people. This bond is so strong in Turkey that the Phantom's nickname is Baba, meaning Father. Those who served and flew with the Phantom trusted it – they had faith that the Phantom would never let them down and would bring crews home safely.

Few aircraft have served in an air force for 50 years. The TurAF celebrated the living legend's big anniversary with a series of events. These events also include firsts for Türkiye. The first of these events was an air-to-air photography session on November 15. What makes this shoot different is that for the first time, civilian photographers had the chance to photograph the Phantom from the open ramp of a cargo aircraft.

The session began with a briefing held at the 111 Filo Komutanlığı. Phantom pilots, photographers and the A400M team came together to plan the flight and shoot. The bad weather was the most challenging element, making it necessary to stay below 10,000ft in order for the cargo ramp to be open. However, it was possible to go below the cloud in and around Lake Beyşehir, which is 160 miles from Eskişehir.

Another difficulty was that the ramp-open speed limit of the A400M and the minimum steady flight speed of the F-4E Phantom were very close to each other. It was challenging to adjust the positions of both the A400M and the Phantoms without getting into each other's jet wash. This also limited manoeuvres. Another disadvantage of jet wash is that it distorts the clarity of a photo. To avoid this, the Phantoms mostly flew at lower altitudes than the A400M. The photo shoot was carried out at a speed of between 180 and 200kts at altitudes of 8,000 to 10,000ft.

Another first, on November 16, was that low-level flight training was followed by photographers for the first time. There is no fixed low-level flight training area in Türkiye. Pilots use different valleys for this purpose, depending on the type of mission and aircraft type. These valleys are generally in the Aegean and Eastern Anatolia. Eskişehir is a city built on a plain; it is difficult to find a valley nearby. Personnel from 111 Filo scanned the area to find a suitable area for photographers and found a dam on a water reservoir. The width and depth of the valley were ideal for both flying and photography.

Unfortunately, the weather was cloudy on the day of the shoot; the weather reports received before the flight predicted that the clouds would become suitable for flying in the afternoon. A pilot from the squadron was in the area as an observer and gave the necessary approval for the flight to begin at 1430hrs. With the first pass at 1513hrs, an unforgettable experience began for aviation enthusiasts. Two Phantoms made more than 20 passes in just over half an hour and incredible shots were captured by the estimated 350 local and foreign photographers that had gathered in the region.

The next day, on November 17, a 50th anniversary ceremony was held at the 1. Ana Jet Üssü, Eskişehir with the Turkish Air Force Commander in attendance. More than 650 spotters and over 30 journalists, as well as active and retired personnel, attended the event. The ceremony began with the flights of four phantoms, in which the air force commander participated.

After taking off, the Phantoms flew in various formations for half an hour and saluted the spotters upon landing. Air Force Commander Ziya Cemal Kadıoğlu, flying in a specially painted aircraft for this ceremony, arrived at the parking area. Here, he was greeted by the first Turkish Phantom pilot and first Squadron commander, former Air Force Commander, Ergin Celasin.

The ceremony continued in the afternoon with a flight of four Phantoms. After performing various manoeuvres, six more Phantoms were added to those aircraft on the ground. The crowd was saluted by ten planes performing an elephant walk.

The Phantom took its place in Turkish skies with the first squadron established in Eskişehir 50 years ago, and now the only remaining fleet continues its duty with the 111. Filo. The Phantom, which has started a new era in Turkish aviation and will continue to contribute to the country's defence for a while longer.

Current Air Force Commander Ziya Cemal Kadıoğlu greets former Air Forces Commander Ergin Celasin, the first Turkish Phantom pilot

Eighty-six year-old Ergin Celasin was the first commander of 113th Squadron, the first Phantom squadron. The first Phantom that underwent Terminator modernisation was delivered to the 111th Squadron and Celasin made the first flight as the Air Force Commander

Eye to eye with a Phantom from the cargo ramp of an A400M

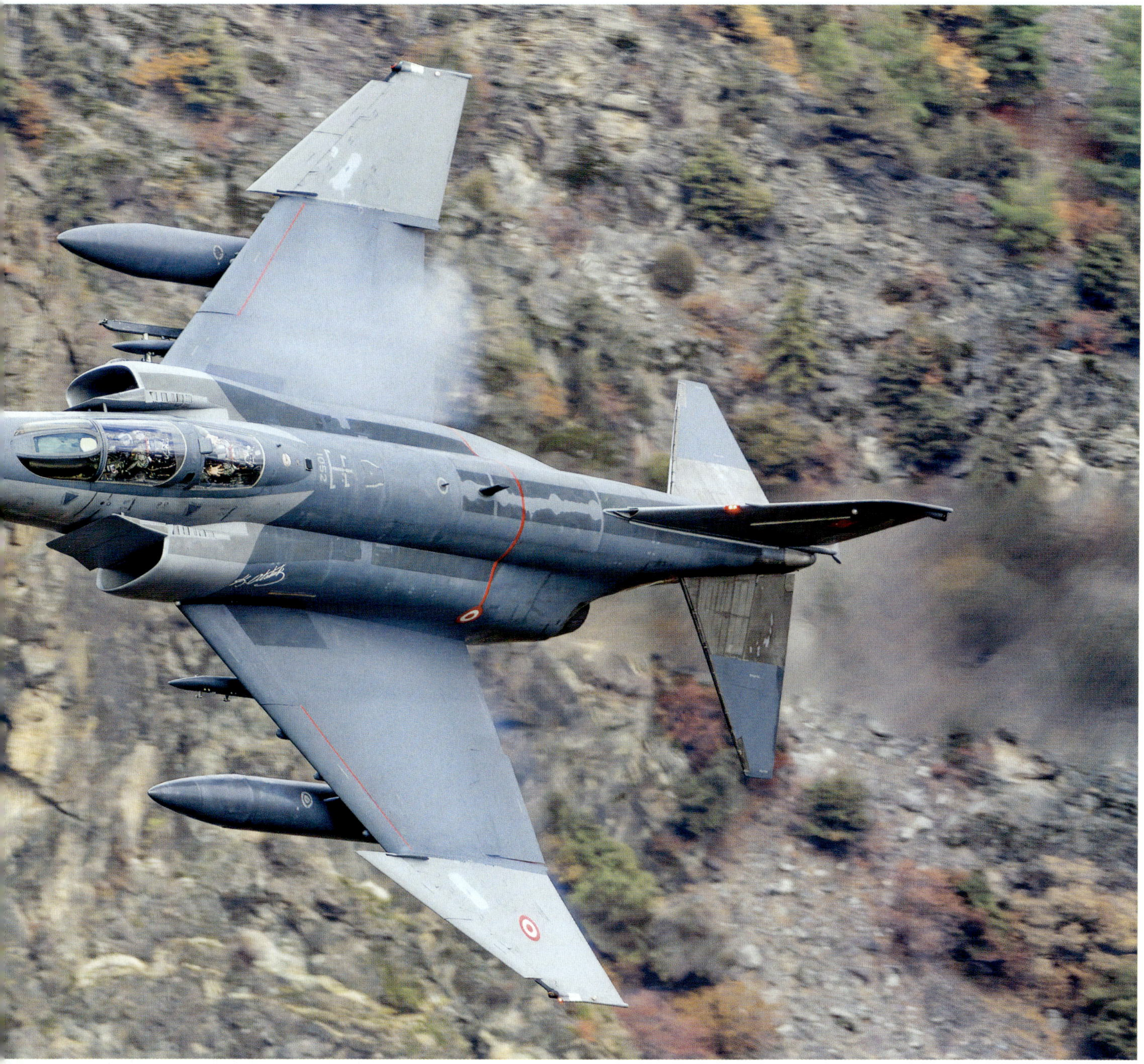

Above: ***While the Phantom pilot shows off his flying skills in the valley, the AKU shows off panther claws. AKU (Arka Kokpit Uçucusu – Rear Cockpit Officer) is the equivalent of Weapon Systems Officer (WSO) in the Turkish Air Force***

Left: ***The Phantom is a unique aircraft whose design consists of angles. The upward slope of the wing and the downward slope of the elevator are easy to see in this photo***

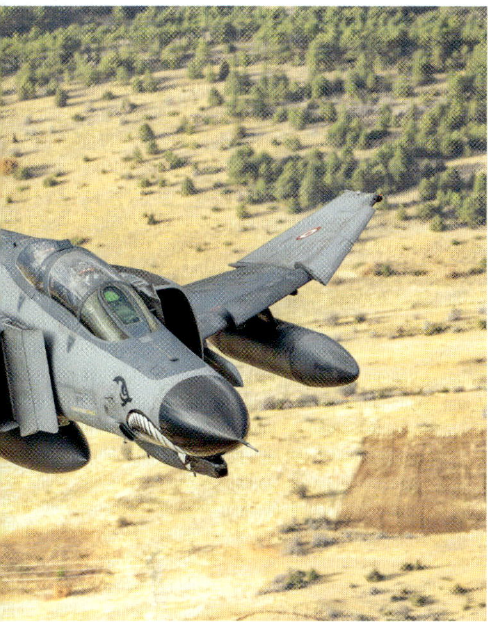

electronic countermeasures (ECM) system, ALQ-119 pods were introduced to increase the electronic warfare capability and protect the aircraft against radar-guided surface-to-air missiles (SAM). Thanks to the APQ-120 radar, which is considered to be the most advanced technology system of its time, the F4E Phantom II can carry out interceptions day and night, in all weather conditions. Thus, the 112th and 172nd squadrons were assigned as an all-weather fighter-interceptor squadron with Sparrow and Sidewinder missiles. Twelve aircraft had TISEO (Target Identification System Electro-Optical), which could fire TV-guided electro-optical missiles 20 to 24 miles from the target.

The TurAF's first encounter with air refuelling was in the Gulf Crisis. With the increasing tension in the region, the number of American tanker aircraft arriving at Incirlik increased rapidly. During this period, the first training of the Phantoms with American tankers began, and the squadrons began to gain air refuelling experience.

Keeping up with the times

Making its maiden flight in 1958, the Phantom represent the technology of the 1960s. Thanks to their standard APQ-120 radar system, the Phantoms successfully carried out air-to-air missions until the mid-80s. However, by the 90s, the existing F-4E Phantom II aircraft in the Turkish Air Force inventory reached high numbers in terms of both airframe life and flight hour rates. Eventually, they became outdated and could not respond to current needs and threats. Turkey had two alternatives

Above: **The Phantom has played an important role in counter-terrorism operations. It is armed with prefragment Mk-82 ammunition which explodes in the air, creating fragmentation across a wide area. This aircraft was seen at Erhac on May 25, 2017**

Right: **73-1026, which was delivered in 1974, was modernised in 2000 and started a new life with the name F-4E/2020 Terminator**

to maintain its strong military position in the region and to increase its deterrence. In line with this need, Turkey would either replace the old Phantom aircraft with a new twin-engine fighter-bomber or upgrade some of the existing F-4E Phantom II aircraft with a comprehensive modernisation project to increase their service life for at least 20 more years. Turkey favoured the modernisation option for economic reasons. Turkey's 30 years of experience in training, equipment, materials, repair, maintenance, and logistic support capability also played a significant role in this decision.

The Israeli Aerospace Industries (IAI) solution, based on the Kurnass 2000 developed for the Israeli Air Force, included the replacement of the existing radar with ELTA product EL/M-2032 and the integration of AN/ALQ-178[V]3 electronic countermeasure system, MXF-484 VHF/ UHF radio, HOTAS flight control system, heads-up display (HUD), integrated INS/ GPS navigation system, airborne videotape recorder (AVTR), full-colour multi-function displays (MFD), a new mission computer and MIL-STD-1553B data bus. Furthermore, the aircraft would gain the ability to fire Popeye-I air-to-surface guided missiles (ASM) and carry ELTA EL/L-8225 electronic warfare pods.

According to the agreement, 26 of the 54 F-4E Phantom aircraft were to be modernised in Israel, and the remaining 28 were to be upgraded in the 1st Air Supply and Maintenance Centre of the Turkish Air

All eyes are on 'her' while this special Phantom taxies past. Atatürk's 'İstikbal Göklerdedir' (The future is in the sky) graphic dominates the tail.

Above: After the Panther and Devil Squadrons merged, the devil's shark mouth became a standard for the Panthers. The Phantom's nose structure is ideal for it

Right: High speed and sharp manouvres combined with the humidity to create an incredible image

Force located in Eskişehir. Israel was to provide the necessary structural and avionic modernisation kits for the 28 jets to be upgraded in Turkey, train Turkish engineers for avionic integration, establish a System Integration Laboratory (SIL), and transfer this laboratory to Eskişehir. Thanks to this technology transfer provided by Israel within the scope of the project, the 1st Air Supply and Maintenance Centre was planned to acquire the capability to carry out the desired structural and avionic changes on the aircraft by improving the technological infrastructure of the centre.

The most significant improvement that increases the strike capability of the Terminators is that the F-4E/2020 aircraft can fire Popeye missiles. The Popeye is a solid rocket-powered stand-off missile weighing 1,360kg (3,000lb) with a 340kg (750lb) blast fragmentation or 360kg (800lb) I-800 penetrating warhead and imaging infrared or TV guidance. It has a reported range of 100km, depending on its launch altitude. The missile can also be controlled directly through the data link.

The first two F-4E/2020 (73-1032 and 68-0498) were delivered to the Turkish Air Force with a ceremony held on January 27, 2000.

During its 50-year long adventure in Turkey, which started on August 30, 1974, Phantoms served in nine different squadrons (111,112,113, 131,132,171,172,173, and 401) and introduced the Turkish Air Force to modern radar, ECM and ammunition. In addition to working with advanced weapon systems, Phantoms had another significant contribution; thanks to the Terminator modernisation projects, the TurAF and Turkish Defence Industry gained unprecedented experience in system integration, product development, and testing procedures. **afm**

The leading edge slats that are unique to late F-4Es allow the Phantom to fly at low speeds and make sharper turns